School

DISCARD

Titles in the *Objekt* series explore a range of types – buildings, products, artefacts – that have captured the imagination of modernist designers, makers and theorists. The objects selected for the series are by no means all modern inventions, but they have in common the fact that they acquired a particular significance in the last 100 years.

School

Catherine Burke and Ian Grosvenor

REAKTION BOOKS

To Mary and David Medd, who in their lives and practice together made the relation of education to architects their 'subject'.

Published by Reaktion Books Ltd
79 Great Sutton Street
London EC1V 0DX, UK

www.reaktionbooks.co.uk

First published 2008

Copyright © Catherine Burke and Ian Grosvenor 2008

Printed and bound in China by Imago

British Library Cataloguing in Publication Data

Grosvenor, Ian
School. – (Objekt)
    1.Educational sociology 2. School buildings
    I. Title II. Burke, Catherine, 1957–
    306.4'3

ISBN-13: 978 1 86189 302 4

Contents

Introduction

The average high school graduate has spent about 13,000 hours within the walls of a public school building. These 13,000 hours are potentially the most impressionable and valuable hours of his life . . . Through this environment . . . the whole costly process of education may be encouraged or nullified. The school building is the tangible and visible evidence of the attitude of the public towards education.

William G. Carr, National Education Association, 1935[1]

'Reading' a school in a landscape is not difficult. Although it may have architectural features in common with other public places and institutions, schools are nevertheless quickly placed and are rarely confused with anything else. While some features of their design may be ubiquitous, schools also display regional and local characteristics in materials, form and style. The sight of a school in the landscape results in many different narratives, depending on the point of view of the onlooker: a child may recognize a safe haven or a place of dread; the teacher will recognize a place where they strive to transform the lives of individuals according to their vocation and professional identity; an older person will remember school-days – the smells, sights and sounds of their school; the architectural historian will recognize design features that betray a particular fashion for certain materials and styles at a particular time and place and the influence of certain architects; the educational historian will ask questions about how the building is located in the larger story of the history of communities and the development of ideas about childhood, teaching and learning. When taking an international viewpoint, the historian will also be interested in the association between schools and the formation of national identity.

Like other buildings, schools are the products of social behaviour. They should not be viewed merely as capsules in which education is located and teachers and pupils perform, but also as designed spaces that, in their materiality, project a system of values. In turn, the ways in which the buildings are used and experienced give them meaning. But is it possible to look at a building and see it as the architect and others did in the past and to recover their experience of it? The answer can be only a tentative and partial yes. First, in the search for meaning we need to bring the subject and object, both historically located, together in the same narrative.[2] Such a narrative begins with the moment of a building's conception and continues through its design, construction and use – concluding, in some cases, in its eventual destruction – and it should try to include the views of all those involved in each of these stages.

Schools inevitably change over time and with use. For example, a school may start out as a mixed elementary school, then take boys only; it may shift age range and return to being mixed; it may be closed and then reopened as a community facility or designer home. Externally, very little changes, but internally notices appear, walls are removed, offices and corridors created and classrooms knocked through. The school exists in a sea of pupils and parents, and although it remains the same, its position in the landscape may alter substantially, caused by local population exodus, building intensification, community regeneration or the arrival of new communities. Whatever the school's new name and function, it will still appear to be either what it looks like – a late nineteenth-century Board school, a 1960s comprehensive school, a Victorian infants' annexe – or what the locals have always called it – its original or vernacular name.

'Schools into homes 2006-7'. This development in Birmingham, England uses the 'shell' of the former Severn Street School, the city's first Nonconformist school, started in 1809. The First Day School was opened on this site in 1845 and was founded by the Quaker merchant, anti-slavery and peace campaigner Joseph Sturge to teach adults and poor children.

This book is designed to reveal the ways in which schools, through their initial design and subsequent re-shaping through habitation, make clear their function in society as fragmented sites of cultural memory and creation. Our subject reflects a contemporary and growing interdisciplinary and international interest in matters of space and place in education. Rather than viewing the school building – its various rooms, walls, windows, doors and furniture, together with outdoor 'nooks and crannies', gardens and open spaces – as a neutral or passive 'container', architects and educators have considered it to be an *active agent*, shaping the experience of schooling and promoting and even pioneering a particular understanding of education. Certain aspects of what makes a school, such as halls, corridors, playgrounds and classrooms, have taken differents form through time. Such factors as the design of school furniture can be seen to reflect pervasive notions of pedagogy, but also to promote ideas and theories about the relationship between pupil and teacher and between body and mind in learning. Design features that permit observation and surveillance – controlling, ordering and disciplining children within the school walls – have always been crucial, and continue to be part of modern schooling, and they have always exploited technological developments, for example chairs designed to control posture. Legislation and government agendas for education have shaped schools and given substance to their role in the community. At different times, teachers, advisers, architects and designers have realized their unity of purpose in designing schools to fit the needs of children and the wider society.

Whatever the type of school, a group of people comes together to design a structure based upon ideas about what the teacher or learner should be doing when they interact. It is these ideas that create classrooms, situate corridors and locate specialist rooms, common spaces and surrounding areas in particular ways. Apart from the usual limitations that result from planning regulations and local requirements, and in a much more fundamental way, the group's collective experience acts as a limitation on its capacity to imagine a different educational future. In this sense, each school site is a compound of imagination, reaction, sedimentation or radical intervention in education. Lighting, room shape, access to the outside and common spaces, for example, are reflections of contemporary thought about learning and teaching. They are not just technical solutions, related to cost and supply, but also to views about how teachers and learners in designed spaces should be supported to act, and to what end.

Of course, schools have existed for centuries, sometimes catering for the poor, but mostly for the elite, and often associated with a religious institution. In the past they have been designed to resemble a place of common living for a religious purpose, a place of production (i.e., a factory or an office) or a *domus* (home or

'Contemporary thought about learning and teaching', division, Orphelinat (orphanage) National des Chemins de Fer, Colonie d'Avernes, France, c. 1920.

farm). The domestication of educational spaces has at times been part of a progressive agenda that has seen the comfort, freedom and emotional security of children to be a priority. Thus, the design of school buildings, both the exterior shell and the interior ordering of spaces and furnishings, is in a symbiotic relationship with ideas about childhood, education and community. In general, schools catering for whole populations started out as single-room buildings for mixed-age groupings. Gradually, the idea of separating the ages and sexes and having separate rooms for specialist subjects emerged as the norm. As cities developed, large multi-storey municipal buildings began to dominate the urban landscape. In London at the end of the nineteenth century, for instance, the new Board schools were built high, since they were situated in densely populated areas where land was at a premium. It was at this time that the idea that the nation state should bear

Schools are inhabited spaces; Malaga, Spain, c. 1955.

the financial and moral burden of educating the masses came to be accepted across most parts of the industrialized world.

Not all schools were purpose-built spaces designed for education. Many occupied buildings designed for other purposes. Private schools took over large private country houses or city villas; rural schools occupied barns or extended cottages; and city schools over-spilled into any available local annexe. For example, the American educational reformer John Dewey opened his 'Laboratory School' at the University of Chicago in 1896. The building was a former residence, and it worked very well for a programme that was built around hands-on learning activities that supported real life. Classrooms were appropriately formed from the former living spaces of the home. Furniture consisted of tables and chairs that could be arranged according to the activity.[3]

Before the coming of mass schooling, public spaces – the market, the church, the theatre – provided learning opportunities for city children. For example, in *Town Swamps and Social Bridges* (1859), a little-known study of London life before mass schooling, George Godwin saw the worrying 'absence of knowledge' as a result of the want of opportunity, and identified 'penny' or street theatre', characterized by 'the singing of popular street songs and negro melodies in characteristic costumes . . . [d]ancing of the most vigorous description . . . feats of strength and conjuring', as the 'the chief means of education to large bodies of boys and girls'. This 'sort of *education* was eagerly taken advantage of.'[4]

In many areas of the world, a school was (and is) reduced to its barest recognizable elements: a single place of meeting, a teacher, a means of instruction, a means of inscription, an organized form of seating (usually arranged in lines), a shared purpose and, of course, children. In some schools, classes had to be held outside. It is only since the mid-nineteenth century that there have been

212. Une École indigène

School in a barn, Potes, northern Spain, photographed in 2001.

'School without walls': North Africa, end of the nineteenth century.

large-scale changes in school provision, involving several distinct stages of active reconsideration and redesign. Such waves of activity brought architects and educators together, often supported by their respective governments, to seek for themselves innovative answers to the question of the school. At such times, whole nations have been keenly interested in the achievements of their neighbours.

While all nation states have a history of school building, closely linked to the demographics and politics of the region, *School* focuses on Western school building and is organized around four defining periods – the late nineteenth century, the early to mid-twentieth century, the mid- to late twentieth century, and the present. These reflect general trends, respectively the period in which schooling systems were established; the expansion of mass systems of education; the challenge to traditional forms of education; and finally, the question of school futures, where learning has

Jardin de Infantes Integral, 'Antonio Aberastain' (kindergarten), Barracas, Buenos Aires, built in the 1950s.

shifted beyond traditional sites and where the nature of knowledge is uncertain.

In the second half of the nineteenth century nation states created organized means of governing, and education was systematized and funded by means of regulation, training and design. This was the moment when the establishment of a national education system that was free, compulsory and designed for the masses was a fundamental sign of industrial, commercial and political maturity. State education, the origins of which go back to the Calvinist and Lutheran Reformations in the sixteenth century, was first established in

A 'Plan 60' school in Buenos Aires built in the period 1976–83. The school, one of 60 planned by the military dictatorship, was built by the city council using private studios of architects.

modern form in Prussia during the first half of the nineteenth century, and extended to the rest of the nation after the formation of the German state. The form that schooling took in the militarily powerful Prussian state became a model for most modernizing nations. France, for example, had experimented with state regulation and the control of public schooling during the revolutionary and Napoleonic eras, but it was not until its military defeat by Prussia in 1871 that it set about matching that state's education system in an attempt to revitalize itself. Most countries in Europe had established compulsory education by 1900, with the exception of Belgium, which followed by 1920.

Many aspects of a society and its government were made clear to its citizens through the establishment of these specialist sites of instruction. Pupils learned their place in the world; they were graded and selected; they learned systems of classification, and studied objects from the locality, the country and the world. It was at school that they were taught their responsibilities, their duty and their sense of place. They were to learn through an organized curriculum, with special resources and technologies, including dedicated rooms. Schools were designed to help this mass of pupils manage this task, and as the scope of the task increased, as education became more complex, the design of the school, its function and the technologies it enclosed became more complicated. Laboratories, art rooms and gymnasiums had to be built or their specialist equipment inserted into older buildings. The cost of schooling meant that school design and construction became a specialized area of planning, and exchange of information about solutions to technical and production problems took place inside countries and even between them.

In the United States, the colonies of New England led the way in education, influenced by the Puritan origins of the first settlers.

The Quakers opened schools for all faiths and German settlers erected buildings to house schools. Benjamin Franklin (1706–1790), a leading advocate of the power of education in building nationhood, established the Philadelphia Academy and a free charity school in 1751. Franklin also founded a school for black people, free and un-free, which opened in 1758.[5] By 1850 there were approximately 6,000 academies in existence and all the American states had public (i.e., state) schools, with Massachusetts and Connecticut already imposing compulsion. High schools began to emerge in the nineteenth century, as an extension of the 'common school'. The Civil War, which finally ended in 1865, severely disrupted the development of society, and the second half of the nineteenth century was characterized by a pedagogy of nation building. Both rural and urban typologies of building style were established: in the warm climates of the South, schools could

Old German School, Philadelphia, 1761, architect Robert Smith (1722–1777).

be found in informal outdoor settings, such as gazebos or open structures that provided shade. By 1900 all American states had enforced compulsory school attendance and a standardized building plan had emerged under the pressure of large-scale immigration. 'The creation of standardized building plans paralleled efforts to further standardize the school curriculum and continuing efforts to "Americanize" the diverse student population.'[6]

The end of the nineteenth century was an extraordinarily productive time, when many large urban schools were designed and constructed across Europe and the Americas. The insistence that whole populations of children should be educated demanded considerable investment in capital building projects. In Europe, the numbers of children attending school increased from around a quarter of the child population in 1870 to close to three-quarters by 1900.[7] In the USA, less than 50 per cent of children (aged between 5 and 17) attended school before 1870, and for those who did attend, as in Europe, the school year was very short.[8] Private schools independent of the state were permitted to coexist in most places in Europe and North America, but a significant characteristic of the time was that the state created a role for itself in maintaining quality and regulating those schools outside its immediate control.

The second period of reflection, change and school-building activity occurred in Europe following the First World War. These decades were characterized by social democratic politics of health and hygiene, and major shifts in educational theory and policy, while architects were influenced by the Modernist movement. There was an emphasis on lighting, a shift from monumental to functional design and a move towards recognizing the scale at which the small child operated. Experimental pedagogies were evident in Europe and the United States as schools with 'alternative' or 'progressive' philosophies and practices became established, drawing on new forms of knowledge emerging from the psychological and educational disciplines. This period saw a reconsideration of the view of the child through the impact of new ideas about child development, and this, of course, impacted on the way that the school was physically organized. There was continued expansion in the numbers of children receiving some form of education and the extent of that period of study. In the USA, for example, 32 per cent of children between the ages 14 and 17 received some form of education in 1920, but this had increased to 73 per cent by 1940.[9]

The Second World War, the demands of reconstruction and significant population growth led to a third wave of activity. This stimulated further reconsideration of what 'school' might be in Europe and the United States, which led to an important period of experimentation and innovation that lasted until the 1960s. The major concern in the post-war world was how education might be renewed as a force to secure democracy. Post-Fascist states such as Italy made important efforts to build democratic communities, starting with a renewal of the pre-school environment. Important advances were made in the United States to abolish the segregation of black and white pupils in separate schools, a vital component of the civil rights movement. In many Western democracies, the comprehensive ideal of schooling took firm hold in a climate where equality and challenges to past hierarchical structures of power were thought to enhance the involvement of communities in reconstruction and planning for peace. The scale of rebuilding was large, since the post-war 'baby boom' placed unprecedented demands on these countries. The response needed to meet the demand stimulated experimentation and collaboration, and resulted in a climate of innovation in school design and pedagogies. During the last two decades of the twentieth century there was a return to traditional schooling strategies and hierarchies, as Western governments reconstructed themselves in the context of a post-industrial market economy.

In this first decade of the new millennium there is reappraisal of what the school should or could be, particularly in the light of the challenges and opportunities posed by the development of the World Wide Web and related information and communication technologies. There is a possibility that the school as we have known it, established in the nineteenth and twentieth centuries, with a subject-based curriculum delivered didactically in traditional classrooms, is disappearing, as learning anything, anywhere and at any time is becoming potentially achievable. Everything that was once stable and unquestioned is being challenged – the traditional role of the teacher; the concept of knowledge as established, secure and transmittable; the place of schools in the community; and the role of the state in directing mass education. At the same time, there is a counter-emergence of traditional formulas, arrangements and beliefs, stimulated by a loosening of the relationship between school and state. This is creating an educational market that draws sustenance from popular anxieties about changes in the social and cultural context of childhood and family.

Of course, as with all historical divisions these boundaries are artificial, and the different phases of change mask elements of continuity. There is a marked continuity in the form that schooling has taken in the modern era and a consistency across cultures of certain reoccurring anxieties. These anxieties are revealed through focusing on the physical context of the school, the design of the buildings and the interior fashioning of its spaces. For example, concerns about children's bodies and general constitution are reflected time and again in food and in the designs for windows, playgrounds, play equipment and furniture. Anxieties about the control and disciplining of large numbers of individuals, both children and adults, within the institution are reflected through discussions about the arrangement of classrooms, corridors, stairwells, gates and fences, and, latterly, the installation and positioning of security cameras. The opening to the wider community has conflicted with anxieties about risk and the provision of a safe haven for children, and school buildings have altered considerably over time in response to health and safety regulations. For example, the numbers of school entrances and exits have been reduced in recent years and security fences are commonplace around the newest buildings. A recent poll of schoolchildren concerning their sense of security at school returned a surprisingly large number of respondents who felt over-protected and that their schools were beginning to resemble prisons.[10]

New building materials (concrete, steel, electronically controlled gates) and the development of furniture materials (tubular steel, plywood, plastic) have changed the construction, interior look and physical feel of schools. Modernist designers, such as Piet Zwart and Ferdinand Kramer (1920s); Henri Liber and Pierre Chareau (1930s); Jean Prouvé (1940s); Friso Kramer and Robin Day (1950s); Roberto Pamio, Borge Lindau and Bo Lindekrantz (1960s); and Marc Berthier (1970s), all experimented with the design of the classroom table and chair.[11] Changes in furniture design were accompanied by new ideas about pedagogy and learning styles. Desks with attached seats (oak and cast iron) were replaced by tables and individual chairs (wood/plastic and tubular steel), which offered greater scope for group work and pupil interaction. Their introduction reconfigured the classroom space, since tables and particularly chairs could be stacked for more flexible use. Some schools, in rural parts of Sweden for example, even used adjustable furnishings to offer a more 'comfortable fit', to take the

different physiques of pupils into account. Of course, new classroom furniture did not come cost-free, so it not surprising to find photographs of schools and even individual classrooms clearly in a state of furniture transition – a mixture of different styles, designs and sizes of chairs, tables and desks being commonplace.

However, while there has been an interest in experimenting with design throughout all four periods, any widespread introduction of ergonomic school furniture has failed to materialize. Cost, the nature of supply through the contract-furniture industry, the predominance of traditional ideas about classroom practice and the failure to listen to children's views have all been factors here. Concern with the poor quality of school furnishings was articulated as early as 1743, when a French orthopaedic physician, Nicholas Andry de Bois-Regard, warned about body deformities as

Primary school, Mexico City, 1980s.

a consequence of stressful postures: 'Most part of Children have their bodies made crooked in learning to write, because people are not at pains to give them a Table high enough for the purpose.'[12] Such concerns have since appeared regularly. The first architect of the London School Board, E. R. Robson, included a chapter on furniture in his *School Architecture*, first published in 1838; furniture was a feature of education exhibitions throughout the twentieth century; and in 2002 the Design Council in Britain produced a report entitled *Kit for Purpose: Design to Deliver Creative Learning*, which documented how in the UK nearly £1 billion a year was spent on educational resources, but much of what was purchased was 'poorly designed, standardized and well behind adult workplaces'.[13]

As historians of education we recognize that we are equally open to the charge levelled at an earlier account of school architecture – of being 'outsiders to the sub-culture which architects inhabit' and being prone as 'professional educational pundits' to believe that 'Form follows Curriculum'; that it is educational innovation that generates architectural progress in school building.[14] This book is by no means intended as a comprehensive history of school architecture and educational design, as it is mainly concerned with state education, and has been conceived as a series of case studies within a narrative framework to demonstrate continuities and discontinuities in architectural history; the interconnectedness of progressive ideas in design and education; and the passion with which a concern for educating the child can absorb not just teachers and other educators but also become the 'subject' of an architectural life. Clearly, in realizing this agenda we have had to be selective in the stories we tell about individual schools, and we are conscious that we might be accused of bias towards the local (English) as against the international in this selection. That said, this English dimension acts as a unifying thread running through the text, and the schools we write about are all, for one reason or another, recognized as iconic in the history of school design.

1 Beacons of Civilization

> If popular education be worth its great price, its houses deserve
> something more than a passing thought. School-houses are hence-
> forth to take rank as public buildings, and should be planned and
> built in a manner befitting their new dignity.
> Edward R. Robson (1874)[1]

In the *Strand Magazine* of 1893 Arthur Conan Doyle has the
detective Sherlock Holmes looking across London's landscape and
observing to Dr Watson:

> 'Look at those big, isolated clumps of buildings rising up
> above the slates, like brick islands in a lead-coloured sea.'
> 'The Board schools.'
> 'Lighthouses, my boy! Beacons of the future! Capsules with
> hundreds of bright little seeds in each, out of which will spring
> the wiser, better England, of the future . . . '[2]

The Board schools had been established under the Elementary
Education Act of 1870 with the express purpose of extending the
education available to working-class children into a national system operating through local school boards. The sentiments behind
the frequently quoted exchange between Holmes and Watson –
schools as civilizing sites for the masses – were not unique to
either Conan Doyle or England. In Spain, graded schools, which
provided education for children between 5 and 13 years grouped
by age and level of knowledge in different classrooms, first opened
in Cartagena, Murcia, in 1903, and were promoted as embodying

the 'wisdom of progress', as 'palace[s] of education' and true mon-
uments 'raised in honour of national culture'. In the USA in the
same decade educational reformers argued that schools of any
community were 'gauges of its enlightenment'.[3] Nor were these
sentiments confined to the late nineteenth and early twentieth
centuries. As early as 1816 a report in England pointed to the critical importance of schools as a factor in improving 'the general
civilization' of the industrializing nations, and in the 1930s the
architect Werner Moser argued that the school should be 'the dominant element of the group of constructions' that surrounded it
and the 'symbol' of culture.[4] What is unique, of course, is Conan
Doyle's language, in particular, his use of a vocabulary commonly
associated with the construction of buildings, whether materials
(slates, bricks, lead), type (houses, lighthouses, beacons, schools) or
design (capsule). However, would the architects of Holmes's
'Beacons' have used the same language to describe their creations?
The French architect J.N.L. Durand had proposed earlier in the

Bonner Street Primary School, Bethnal Green, London, 1876; architect E. R. Robson.

century that a set of principles and elements could be extracted from architecture to create a commonly understood and agreed 'grammar' of architecture whereby students could be given 'the means of composing all kinds of buildings'.[5] Would there have been then, for example, a shared understanding of the word 'capsule'? What other language would have been in this grammar? Would nineteenth-century architects have talked about or even understood the phrase 'educational space'?

These questions act as a reminder that the practice of history today often involves a reading of the past that is shaped by present concerns and understandings. For example, it is an emerging practice amongst those investigating the impact of the built environment on individuals and groups to describe it in terms of the production of space, as an interaction between the physical and the social.[6] Thus, the questions we ask at present, the ways we make sense of buildings and spaces and the understandings we generate would not necessarily be recognized or understood as part of past practices, grammars and vocabularies. What, then, can be said about the Board schools, the Spanish first-grade schools and other schools that appeared on the education landscape to cater for the masses in the late nineteenth century? In order to answer this question, it is necessary first to consider how these new 'modern' schools for the masses emerged.

The accelerated processes of modernization experienced in western Europe and North America in the later stages of the nineteenth century demanded rapid accommodation to new conditions. Major transformations in economic and industrial structures and technological advancements led to the growth of cities, caused by concentrated capital and mass migration to enlarge the workforce. Work and workers were 're-made' as labour processes were broken down, rationalized into component activities and reassembled into

Cranbook Road Board School, London, *Art Journal* (1881).

Jedonian Road Board School, London, *Art Journal* (1878).

efficient production units. Economic and industrial developments increasingly involved the state in planning and managing change. Work, schooling, family life and leisure increasingly became the objects of surveillance – life experiences were classified and documented – as technologies of the social evolved. Medical science expanded with the emergence of psychiatry and the movement for measuring and classifying intelligence and disorders scientifically. Norms of social behaviour were imposed on all spheres of social life, and individuals were increasingly expected to conform to broader socio-political objectives. The emergence of mass democracy in the advanced capitalist states was matched by increased consumption and the development of intensely nationalistic ideologies. The move towards universal adult suffrage caused concern among the political elite that their power might be eroded by an uneducated electorate exercising choice. Rapid and vast technological innovation brought with it the anger of unrest or the threat of revolution, and mass education was regarded as one means to avoid this.

Initially, schooling for the masses came in all sorts of forms. In England, Sunday schools, an idea popularized first by Anglicans and then by Protestant dissenters in the last years of the eighteenth century, promoted basic literacy amongst working-class children, but not writing: the former provided access to the Bible, but the latter risked promoting sedition. Sunday schools operated in chapels, mills, converted houses and barns, and gradually spread throughout England to Scotland and Wales. The first purpose-built Sunday school housed the Hoxton Methodist Sunday School in Bethnal Green, London. Built in 1802, the two-storey structure accommodated 1,000 pupils, with boys and girls on different floors. Each floor could be organized as a single large room for singing and prayer or subdivided with wooden partitions for literacy lessons. The large single schoolroom gradually became a feature of Sunday school buildings.[7] Another site of working-class schooling was the 'ragged school', which emerged out of the Sunday school movement. Located in rooms in the slum areas of English cities, these charged no fees and aimed to meet the needs of abandoned or neglected children, whether that involved providing a very basic education or simply taking homeless children off the streets. In the mid-nineteenth century there were 82 such schools in London alone, educating more than 17,000 children. The conditions in these schools were often very poor, as Charles Dickens described on a visit to Field Lane Ragged School in the Clerkenwell area of London on a Thursday evening in September 1843:

> The school is held in three most wretched rooms on the first floor of a rotten house; every plank, and timber, and lath, and piece of plaster in which shakes as you walk. One room is devoted to the girls: two to the boys . . . I have very seldom seen, in all the strange and dreadful things I have seen in London and elsewhere, anything so shocking as the dire neglect of soul and body exhibited in these children . . .
>
> The school is miserably poor . . . and is almost entirely supported by the teachers themselves . . . The moral courage of the teachers is beyond all praise. They are surrounded by every possible adversity, and every disheartening circumstance that can be imagined. Their office is worthy of the apostles.[8]

The idea of extending education to the poor was also exported to other cities in the British Empire, and a ragged school opened in Sydney, Australia, as late as 1860.[9] Other schools in England were located in factories, and there were others inside workhouses for the poor.[10] The voices of working-class children in this period rarely survive. In his autobiography, Thomas Wood, an engineer, remembered attending a factory school as a boy in Bingley, Yorkshire, in the 1830s:

> It was a cottage at the entrance to the mill yard. The teacher, a poor old man who had done odd jobs of a simple kind for about 12s a week was set to teach the half-timers [children who worked in the mill as well as attending school]. Lest, however, he should teach too much or the process be too costly he had to stamp washers out of cloth with a heavy wooden mallet on a large block of wood during school hours.[11]

In both urban and rural areas it was a fairly simple matter for a literate working man to set up a school; all he needed was to declare his front room to be a school and gain the support of local parents. Unmarried women also opened their houses and gardens to children for small fees. These 'dame' schools were a common feature in rural environments. In the 1830s more than half of all elementary education was unsystematized and unregulated.[12]

By the mid-nineteenth century there were more than 11,000 parish schools in England and Wales, educating over 1.5 million pupils.[13] Publications such as *The Ecclesiologist*, Henry Kendall's *Designs for Schools and School Houses* (1847) and William Butterfield's *Instrumenta Ecclesiastica* (1852) took an interest in the designs of these little buildings, for which they advocated the Gothic Revival style. *The Ecclesiologist* noted that the school should be the 'prettiest building in the village, next to the church', and in an article of 1847 it recommended that the schoolroom and the schoolmaster's house should be set at right-angles to one another, roofed separately and with a lean-to cloakroom. Gothic details, however, had already been used by A.W.N. Pugin at his 1841 Roman Catholic parish school at Spetchley, Worcestershire, combined with vernacular materials. This simple rustic building, built of red brick, has a picturesque skyline with gabled roof, mullioned windows and projecting chimneystack and bellcote. A two-storey master's house is attached at the side. Buildings of similar character were subsequently erected by such High Anglican architects as Butterfield, William White (Probus, Cornwall, 1849) and G. E. Street (Inkpen, Berkshire, 1850). Cramped sites in towns necessitated multi-storey buildings, as in J. W. Wild's Northern District School of St Martin-in-the-Fields, London (1849–50), which had classrooms on the first two floors and a covered playground on the top storey, which was articulated with Gothic arcades. Built in brick, its novel Italianate style was praised by Ruskin and proved influential in many secular buildings.[14]

At the very end of the eighteenth century, education for working-class children was significantly extended in England with the development of the monitorial system. This was the result of a growing interest in the idea that human nature was transformable, especially in childhood, and of increasing demographic pressure as a consequence of industrialization and urban growth. The system involved a radical change in the design of the schoolroom in order to educate the largest number of children at the least expense. The credit for its development was claimed by two educational reformers, the Anglican Dr Andrew Bell (1752–1832) and the Nonconformist Dr Joseph Lancaster (1776–1838), each of whom accused the other of plagiarism. Whatever its origins, the monitorial system involved the subdivision of a single space – a large or smaller-sized rectangular schoolroom – to allow for 'mutual education'. This mechanical system enabled very large numbers to be schooled in spaces under the single gaze of one master by means of monitors spread around the class – pupils who instructed small groups of children through drill and repetition. Lancaster's *Hints and Directions for*

SECTION

1.—LANCASTERIAN SCHOOL.

Building, Fitting Up and Arranging School Rooms (1809) set out
the technical and human requirements of the system. Two types
of school structures were dominant: smaller single-room schools
in rural areas, such as the one at West Wittering in southern
England (now part of the Weald and Downland Open Air Museum
in rural Sussex), and large urban halls, often two or three storeys
in height, containing hundreds of scholars. Lancaster elaborated
further on his plan in 1811, producing 'guidance' for a builder for
a single schoolroom measuring 70 by 32 feet. Designed to accommodate 320 pupils, it contained twenty rows of desks and forms
arranged to face a master on a raised platform, and set out to
enable the pupil-monitors to move easily between the rows. Floor
space was left at the sides of the room to enable the children to
stand in semicircles facing the walls, on which lesson boards were
hung. Lancaster was against the inclusion of a ceiling in the
schoolroom because this would trap the high noise levels caused
by the monitors questioning children in their groups. The school
was to be equipped with four water closets and three urinal stalls
housed in a small yard outside.[15]

A one-room eighteenth-century school, West Wittering, Sussex.

'Lancasterian School', woodcut, c. 1874.

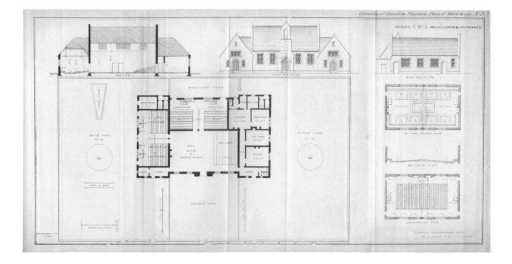

The general principles behind Lancaster's school design and the monitorial system were further developed by other educationalists, who were similarly concerned with the problems associated with popular education. The single-room school operated a system in which monitors kept pupils under constant surveillance and were in turn watched by the master. Pupil time was organized systematically. Pedagogy structured the space inhabited by the master, the head monitor, monitors, assistant monitors and children. Instruction and control flowed through a series of relays. Groups of children were separated into class rows or blocks based on achievement; through success or failure in competition, the children were continuously able to change their positions. Handbooks elaborated the teaching methods to be employed, the location of school equipment and the nature of child posture and gestures to be expected. As Thomas Dunning observed, however, the monitorial system did not necessarily advance the learning of the more able children:

'Committee of Council on Education, Plans of School-houses No. 12', for 144 children and 150 infants (1839/40).

I was sent to . . . [a] school on Bell's system, to learn but very little. The boys who could read moderately well were appointed to teach the younger or lower classes. I was one of these and I had very little time allowed me for either writing or arithmetic, and none for grammar or geography.[16]

The monitorial system was modified under the influence of Samuel Wilderspin and David Stow in the 1820s and '30s. Wilderspin was particularly concerned with the teaching of infant children. In his model school in Spitalfields, London, he introduced a separate room for a 'class' of children opening off the schoolroom; the master could teach each class in turn, while the mistress supervised the other children:

The class that has done first is taken into a separate room, where the children have each another lesson, though in a different way from the first, for in what we call the class room, the children being formed into a square all say their lessons together.[17]

This structural division of the school space enabled a new form of pedagogy to evolve, that of the 'simultaneous method', in which the master instructed all the children in the room at the same time. Wilderspin had pictures fixed on poles in the schoolroom so that all the children could see them, but he also introduced a structural change into the schoolroom itself so that the simultaneous method could be employed:

Whatever children can see excites their interest, and this led to the idea of grouping them together, to receive what are called 'object lessons'. First, they were placed at the end of the room, but this was inconvenient; parallel lines were then drawn in chalk across the room, and they

sat down in order on these; but, though the attention was arrested, the posture was unfavourable; some pieces of cord were afterwards placed across to keep them in rank and file, but as this led to a see-sawing motion it was discontinued; I then made various experiments with seats, but did not succeed, until at length, the construction of a gallery, or succession of steps, the youngest occupying the lower and the eldest the higher, answered the desired end.[18]

Wilderspin's gallery was further developed by David Stow in the 1830s, when he introduced into his model school at Glasgow 'a gallery' to seat the whole school. This permitted 'the children to fix their eye more easily upon the master' and enabled 'the master to observe and direct more perfectly every movement of the children'.[19] Unlike Lancaster schools, where the schoolroom sloped so that the master could see all the children, Wilderspin and Stowe altered the floor so that the children could see the master.

Order, discipline and habit formation were fostered through design. For Wilderspin and Stow this extended to the playground,

'Wilderspin's Gallery': S. Wilderspin, *A System for the Education of the Young* (1840).

where children were to be continually under the surveillance of the teacher, and periodically the head teacher. The playground could also function as a moral training ground. Wilderspin described the playground as the space 'where the little children are left to themselves' and where 'it may be seen what effects their education has produced'. His playground, equipped with circular swings on which the children could exercise, was designed to develop their moral behaviour through shared play. He also planted all his playgrounds with fruit trees, which offered both a temptation to children and an incentive to self-regulation. He stated before a Select Committee:

> that is the way in which we endeavour to appeal to the child's judgement; he moves in a society of trained beings, and the next time he stops and looks at a fine cherry he looks about to see whether there is anybody within view. Doubtless he is restrained from taking the cherry by fear, but in process of time, by moving among restrained playfellows, he has command over himself which enables him to resist temptation.[20]

The playground was thus both a space of practised self-restraint and an evidence site for educational success or failure. Stow similarly characterized the playground as 'the uncovered school-room . . . a little world of real life . . . where moral habits can best be formed'.[21]

Schools designed to support the monitorial methods of teaching and discipline and the systematic organization of pupil time also appeared in Canada, Sweden, Russia, France, Barbados, the Netherlands, South Africa and Venezuela. Lancaster schools were built in Philadelphia, New York and Baltimore, the last being established by Lancaster himself following his emigration to America in 1821.[22] What then of other schooling in the United States at this

time? In essence there was a similar pattern of provision as in England, with children at the beginning of the nineteenth century being educated in church basements, rooms in private houses and in one-room schoolhouses. Schoolhouses were generally basic plain wooden constructions, with an assortment of benches, chairs and desks for the children, a teacher's desk at the front with a blackboard, and irregular-shaped windows that admitted a limited amount of light and air. Even the simplest buildings showed the influence of European neo-medieval styles. It was in the rapidly expanding urban areas that schools based on the Lancaster system were introduced. As in England and elsewhere, these were gradually adapted as school administrators introduced ushers to assist the master teacher, often operating in rooms adjacent to the large schoolroom where students recited their lessons.[23] Educational administrators and reformers, such as Horace Mann and Henry Barnard, campaigned for the introduction of a graded system of instruction based on the Prussian method of education and for the replacement of the wood-frame

French monitorial school in the rue de Port-Mahon, Paris, 1818.

buildings with sturdier designs. In his *School Architecture* (1838, 1842, 1848), Barnard, the Rhode Island Commissioner of Public Schools, was blunt in his criticism of the traditional schoolhouse: '[they] are, almost universally badly located, exposed to noise, dust and danger of the highway, unattractive, if not positively repulsive in their external and internal experience'. He also advocated the use of a model one-room schoolhouse in rural areas based on a design by Mann, in which windows lined two walls, the teacher's desk was placed at the front in the centre on a raised platform, and the children sat in rows at individual desks.[24]

Barnard was singular in his praise for the Prussian system of education with its graded instruction of children by age, but what of their school designs? Again, in the early nineteenth century, just as in England, there were schools, especially in the back streets of urban areas, that consisted of single rooms. These schools, again as in England, were run by teachers who applied for a licence and offered a curriculum that involved poor children learning the Lutheran catechism by heart and rudimentary literacy skills. In addition, some poor children attended parish schools set up by local churches, and in the late 1820s public elementary schools were established for 'pauper children'. Faced with the challenges of providing mass schooling, education officials and teachers studied the monitorial systems of Bell and Lancaster. Both systems were seen as appropriate and necessary for England, because of a perceived substantially lower level of education amongst the mass of the population, but they were deemed unsuitable for Prussian schools. Rather, one system of teaching was preferred that was to be applied alike to all the children from the youngest to the eldest, a system that involved separate classes in separate rooms. As the English architect E. R. Robson noted:

There is no general school-room. No raised gallery where the child can receive 'simultaneous instruction'. No breaking the business to him gradually. There is a series of classrooms entered from a wide corridor.[25]

It was a system that functioned in buildings where 'careful thought and desire to perfect every arrangement' was evident, where 'usefulness' dominated over 'show', and where 'economy' was studied, but 'needful provisions' were seldom lacking. In Robson's view, the Prussian system of public instruction was almost, if not quite, 'as military as that which governs the army, and the buildings do not escape the *régime*. If Berlin may be described as a vast barracks, German schools may equally be classed as a series of small barracks', but the designs of schools and the systems used in them were, as Robson critically recognized, 'the real sources of the wealth and progress of the nation and the individual'. They offered lessons for English educationalists and school architects alike.[26]

Robson, the first architect of the London School Board, had undertaken a grand project in the early 1870s to travel through America, Switzerland, Germany, Austria, France, Belgium and the Netherlands 'in search of the best schools' in order to produce a handbook, *School Architecture* (1874), on 'planning and fitting-up school-houses'. There he would have seen some of the imposing urban schools in the imperial capitals, such as the Collège Chaptal in Paris (1865), a three-storey structure in the Second Empire style arranged around three courtyards and the Imperial Gymnasium in Vienna (1865), built in French Gothic, complete with steep roofs and *flèches*.[27]

School Architecture was to show to school founders, school boards and architects 'the various arrangements which may be considered best for health, comfort, and effective teaching of children and . . . how the different parts of the building should fit together so as to form one harmonious whole'.[28] The production of such a handbook was not new – there was Barnard's *School Architecture; or, Contributions to the Improvement of School-Houses in the United States* of 1838 – and Robson was not the last architect to go on an architectural grand tour of school buildings in Europe. Felix Narjoux and Karl Hintrager both later produced panoramic surveys of European school buildings.[29] Robson's book, however, stands out amongst its kind because through it his readers glimpsed not only the situation of existing school buildings and design ideas thought to be iconic as they were emerging across the modern world in the 1860s and '70s, but also a mapping of educational thought and ideas during a period of significant social and political change. Through his travels Robson became keenly aware of how ideas about the design for education were spreading, and his book tells of the spatial dimensions of educational thought. In Germany, he found 'one leading idea', characterized by uniformity in teaching style regardless of the age of the child.[30] In the USA, he discovered detailed knowledge of the English Education Reform Act, even to the extent that this was grasped more securely than by many in England. Through his selection of case-study schools and the narratives constructed around them, Robson provided 'practical and useful' guidance, but in doing so he also helped to determine the parameters of the field of school architecture. Placing this information in a single text, Robson brought together for readers of English designs from across Europe and America. He assembled knowledge from widely dispersed sites and juxtaposed them in new combinations that offered the reader opportunities for reflection, comparison and judgement.

More than this, Robson's trans-national exploration of school architecture also provided a catalyst for a revolution in English school design. The introduction of compulsory education in 1870 had led to the state, both national and local, becoming the agent of change, since a desire for education replaced Bible instruction as a national priority. The task facing cities was enormous, because despite the efforts of organized religion and private bodies, there were not enough school buildings and places in them to meet either the demand for schooling or the numbers of children aged 5 to 13 whom the law now required to be educated. As Robson pointed out, however, architects in England were not well versed in an understanding of what 'educationally' constituted an effective school design. It was, he commented, not a 'subject . . . regarded by architects as possessing much importance'.[31] Robson was very clear on this point – he knew that the audience he had to persuade extended beyond his professional contemporaries to policy-makers. As he wrote in the second paragraph of *School Architecture*: 'there is no complete handbook on planning and fitting-up school-houses . . . [for] school-founders, school-boards, architects and others'. It was these people who recognized that the establishment of a national system of schools for 'the intellectual culture of all classes of the community' was 'of national importance' and that the buildings in which 'the great work . . . [was] to be carried on' should be fit for that purpose. What Robson was determined to provide for this audience as a matter 'of duty' was a book 'strictly practical and useful'.[32] As another architect observed 80 years later, Robson was 'the first educational architect bureaucrat' who was the author of a book 'difficult not to read, period. Argumentative, crusading, self-assured, voraciously well-read, internationally well informed, it is surprisingly readable for a Victorian tract. Zeal is what it has'.[33]

As Robson and his companion John Moss, Secretary to the Sheffield School Board, travelled across Europe, they were assisted in their site visits by industrialists, philanthropists, architects and educationists. In Berlin they met the architect Ernst Ihne, 'the Emperor's architect', who had worked on many important buildings in the city and was able to provide detailed information about the administration of education in the region. They also met Dr Pappenheim, honorary director of a number of kindergartens, who gave them the opportunity to make a surprise visit to a kindergarten in one of the poorer parts of Berlin. Kindergartens were organized to educate young children between the ages of 3 and 6, and were based on the ideas of the German educator Friedrich Froebel (1782–1852), who stressed the importance of music, nature studies, stories and play in promoting learning. Froebel had opened the first kindergarten in Blankenberg in 1837. In 1851 his unorthodox approach to learning led to kindergartens being banned in Prussia, but they were functioning again by the 1860s. At the kindergarten visited by Robson and Moss they witnessed Frobelian pedagogy in practice:

> In the first class-room we found about 50 children seated around low tables and engaged in building up bricks, under the instructions of the teacher. Perfect order prevailed, and the little pupils followed the directions of the teacher with surprising dexterity and perfect regularity, all keeping time to a simple school song.[34]

The kindergarten idea spread to other European countries, North America, the Middle East, Asia and Australia.[35]

Robson visited and later described in detail the Gemeindeschule (Parish or Poor School) in the Kurfüstenstrasse in Berlin, which catered for eligible pre-secondary-school children and was designed by Adolf Gerstenberg, Berlin's chief school architect in the 1860s. The school was built of 'common brick' and consisted of three storeys. There were twelve classrooms in total on the three floors, six for boys and six for girls. In each classroom the windows were located only on one side of the room, that is, to the left of the children, so that their right hands would not cast a shadow. The windows were also placed at a height that would not distract the pupils from their lessons. The teacher's position was on a podium so that he could have a good view of all the children. On the upper floor was a large *aula* (hall), which was used only for public examinations and festivals. There were also teacher's rooms on the two upper floors. The ground floor also housed the living quarters of the headmaster and two reserve classrooms. The cellar contained school accommodation for the janitor, the boiler room and a fuel store. The classrooms for girls and boys and their respective school entrances were separated completely, though men taught both sexes. Each classroom had ample hat pegs arranged in a single line against the wall on two sides, opposite the window and the teachers' platform. The playground consisted of three areas: separate playgrounds for boys and girls and a third area fitted with gymnastic apparatus for use by the boys. The maximum permitted number of children in a class was 60. The Kurfüstenstrasse design was typical of more than 50 other schools built by Gerstenberg.[36] At the Victoria School for Girls in Berlin, Robson and Moss were shown the premises by the director, Dr Haarbricker, and noted the 'careful consideration for the comfort of both scholars and teachers'.[37] While in Chemnitz they visited some very large establishments, one with more than 5,000 pupils. The Koniglisches Gymnasium (Royal Grammar School) had been erected only a year earlier, in 1871–2. Led by the rector, Dr Vogel, Moss reported that they were able to enter classrooms, often unexpectedly, and observe the classes.[38] Moss noted a particularly novel method of writing instruction in one school and in another observed a mathematics lesson. They were helped in their endeavours in Saxony by H. M. Felkin, a British industrialist, who in 1881 published a booklet entitled *Technical Education in a Saxon Town*. The dynamics of these meetings, conversations and guided tours generated networks of contemporaries with common concerns – architecture or education – and their coming together in design.

In the United States, Robson engaged in further conversations and school visits, and found 'a preference for German school plans'. School buildings, often multi-storeyed, containing multiple identical classrooms were a regular feature of the American urban landscape.[39] He commented:

> No people make more determined efforts to obtain information on the subject of schools and schoolhouses from all available sources than those of the United States. The general movement in favour of education is regarded with a deep interest, and in every civilised country the American representative is on the watch to report to Washington the facts concerning any progress which may have been made . . .[40]

He described in detail the 'largest, most costly, and most substantial schoolhouse' erected in America, the High and Normal School-house for Girls in Boston. The school, built in 1870, was five storeys high and accommodated 1,225 pupils. The ground floor had two entrances positioned on opposite sides of the building and connected by a large corridor that also acted as a link to a central hall. Off the central hall were four large classrooms, cloakrooms, six recitation rooms, a waiting room, a library, a teacher's room and a dressing room for female teachers. The storeys above followed a similar arrangement with a hall, classrooms, cloakrooms and recitation rooms. The third storey had a room dedicated to drawing and a cabinet for apparatus. Electric

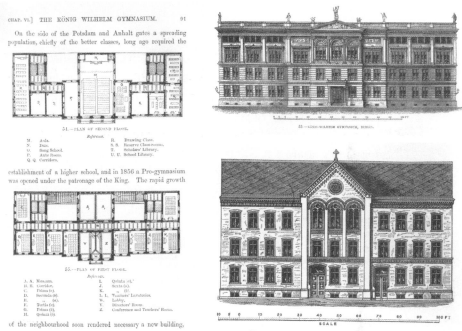

On the side of the Potsdam and Anhalt gates a spreading population, chiefly of the better classes, long ago required the

51.—PLAN OF SECOND FLOOR.

Reference.

M.   Aula.
N.   Dais.
O.   Song School.
P.   Ante Room.
Q. Q. Corridors.

R.   Drawing Class.
S. S. Reserve Class-rooms.
T.   Scholars' Library.
U. U. School Library.

establishment of a higher school, and in 1856 a Pro-gymnasium was opened under the patronage of the King. The rapid growth

55.—PLAN OF FIRST FLOOR.

Reference.

A. A. Museum.
B. B. Corridor.
C.   Prima (a).
D.   Secunda (b).
E.   „   (a).
F.   Tertia (a).
G.   Prima (b).
H.   Quinta (b).

L.   Quinta (a).
J.   Sexta (a).
K.   „   (b).
L. L. Teachers' Lavatories.
W.   Lobby.
Y.   Directors' Room.
Z.   Conference and Teachers' Room.

of the neighbourhood soon rendered necessary a new building,

53.—KÖNIG-WILHELM GYMNASIUM, BERLIN.

46.—PARISH SCHOOL IN THE KURFÜRSTENSTRASSE, BERLIN.

bells and speaking tubes connected the head teacher's room with all the other principal rooms in the school. In the basement there were a central hall, a chemical lecture room, a laboratory, 22 water closets, a boiler room and a room for the janitors. The basement also included a department or 'model' school for primary and grammar school pupils. This department had its own separate entrance, cloakrooms, hall, corridors and toilets. There were two large classrooms with raised platforms for the teacher, and separated fixed seats for the children divided by a gangway. The external design was simple – 'typical', according to Robson, of American school architecture – with pressed brickwork, an ornamented roof, cast-iron cresting, an octagonal turret and with the name of the school cut in large raised letters into the arch stones. The Boston historian E. M. Bacon recorded in 1872 that the turret

Plan and elevation of König-Wilhelm Gymnasium, Belle Vue Strasse, Berlin, c. 1874.

emeindeschule, Kurfüstenstrasse, Berlin; architect Adolf Gerstenberg, c. 1874.

30.—GIRLS' SCHOOL, BOSTON.

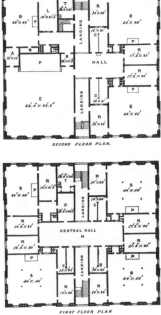

was used as an astronomical observatory and that the central hall contained a 'collection of sculptures and statuary'. Schools such as this one were increasingly seen as having a civic as well as an educational role: the promotion of literacy and numeracy being accompanied by training for life.[41]

At the end of his survey of school plans Robson concluded that what was needed was not to import a design model from abroad, since these were generally 'un-English in spirit and based on systems of training not in favour among us', but to 'think for ourselves in the matter, and so, to speak, build on our own foundations'. At first sight this was a problem. 'History' showed that in the past 'new wants' had been met 'by new developments of the prevalent

The High and Normal School-house for Girls, Boston, Massachusetts, c. 1874.

First and second floor plan.

manner of building', but there had been a decline 'over many years' in England of 'architecture as a vernacular art' and 'consequently, no prevalent architecture of a good type from which to develop'. This decline was a result of the operations of the 'speculative builder', his 'ill-treatment' of his workforce with a consequent 'erasure' of good workmanship, and of divisions amongst architects, which had fostered a 'war of different and conflicting styles'. Robson's solution was to look to the past, before the period of decline, to a time when there was a robust vernacular architecture. That 'foundation' he found in the 'simple brick architecture . . . of the time of the Jameses, Queen Anne, and the early Georges', and within this vernacular frame certain educational and design principles could be enacted. The large schoolroom was not to be abandoned, but, as gradually happened, was to evolve into a large communal hall, rather than continue as a site of regular simultaneous teaching. The other crucial components of school space were cellular classrooms and playgrounds. In bringing these elements – a hall, classrooms and playgrounds – effectively together school architects had to understand the complex and multi-layered interrelationship between subject and object. Buildings had to be designed that promoted 'the method of teaching to be followed' and enabled the teacher to realize their 'best plans of order, classification, discipline and recreation'. The architect had to recognize that the building produced would have to cater for children varying in age, size, gender and studies; that children would be engaged 'sometimes in study and sometimes in recreation'; that 'health and success in study' required daily open air for exercise, good ventilation and controlled temperatures; that seats and desks should be designed with comfort in mind if 'symmetry of form, quality of eyesight, and even duration of life' were not be affected; and that children were impressionable and their 'habits, morals, habits of order, cleanliness and punctuality, temper, love of study and of the school' would be affected by prolonged exposure to the 'attractive or repulsive situation, appearance, out-door convenience and in-door comfort' of the place.[42]

The Queen Anne Revival style came to dominate the London School Board design quickly. It had the advantage of neutrality – it was distinct from both Anglican Gothic and Nonconformist classicism – and facilitated freedom of planning. Robson designed many of the schools himself. Most were built of London yellow stock bricks, with red bricks for the quoins and dressings. Windows had glazing bars and segmental-arched tops, with white-painted frames. The skylines were enlivened by gables and tall chimney-stacks, often with a crowning cupola or bellcote. A notable example is Robson's Bonner Street Primary School in Hackney, built in 1876. A three-storey building, this had the boys' school on top, the girls' in the middle and the infants' on the ground floor.[43]

As Girouard has noted, however, the success of the Queen Anne style led to a 'certain amount of jockeying for the prestige of having invented it'. T. G. Jackson, who had worked with both Robson and John Stevenson, his practice partner, credited Stevenson with being 'the real originator', a role that was also 'believed among architects'. Stevenson himself made similar claims when discussing schools in his *House Architecture* (1880), but, as we have seen, in his memoir of his father, Robson's son was less charitable about Stevenson's creativity. Girouard, with the hindsight of history, credits neither of them, and instead points to Basil Champneys's Harwood Road School of 1872 as being the first Queen Anne Revival-style school in London. What cannot be denied, though, is Robson's critical role in managing the London school building programme (and in later adapting the Queen Anne style in his own designs), which led to the London School Board style. Further, in pursuing this past form of Englishness Robson was not retreating from the present, but attempting to express the modern.[44] Patrick Joyce has argued, following Mitchell Schwarzer, the historian of architectural theory, that the moral shape of the built forms of nineteenth-century cities was historicist. There had developed the idea that every historical phenomenon 'had an individuality and particularity', in which the underlying moral and historical forces that governed the world could be found. In attempting to harness these forces, those engaged in realizing urban character through building design sought to identify the historical forms and styles that best expressed the contemporary understandings of the local and the national. As the identity of the nation and its cities were increasingly understood to be rooted in change, so the emphasis became 'one of becoming, not being', and history was a resource to be tapped both to represent and to give meaning to the modern. In short, 'the historical was a way of being modern'.[45] Robson was part of this process and his book offered ideas about design for mass schooling, the impact of such designs for social relations and their potential both to give meaning to urban life and to act as a mode of indirect governance – the city past and the city present coming together through design.

Education in the Board schools was timetabled into a series of systematized activities, exercises and movements from the start to the finish of each school day, in each week of the school year, for each year of compulsory education. The school bell called children to order at the start of the day. It was time to stop play, to line up in the playground, to enter the school quietly and to begin the process of ordered and regulated learning. Teachers controlled entrance to the school, and pupils entered as subjects of the system. Boys and girls normally entered from separate playgrounds, through separate doorways, each identified by carved brick or terracotta, and along separate staircases. Teachers could move freely through the school. Pupils were faced with areas and spaces that were barred by rules signified by locked doors and signs. Movement was organized to act as a silent form of teaching. The entrances and internal walls of the school carried sculptures, bas-reliefs, moral inscriptions and rolls of honour, all conceived to function as civilizing coercions. The central hall was usually oblong in shape, reflecting the traditional one-room schoolroom design, and was often fitted out to 'realise . . . the combined advantages of isolation and superintendence', with groups of benches and desks arranged along one of its walls and curtains to partition the space when necessary. A report from 1898 captures the continued use of halls as teaching spaces:

> There will be two classes in the hall both either at games or object lessons . . . or at word building or mental arithmetic, the timetable arranging for the occupation of the hall by the different classes in due rotation. There is a distinct gain for young children in the movements thus required . . . it adds to the healthfulness of the school.[46]

Later, the central hall became used increasingly for drill and music lessons as their popularity as school activities increased. It also became a site where the idea of a school as a community could be enacted. Pupils gathered on a daily basis in this space and were managed by teachers to experience the shared rehearsal of moral and religious values.

Classrooms were generally entered from the central schoolroom or hall. The doors to classrooms and the walls separating them were often partially glazed, so that the head of the school could view both teachers and pupils at work and therefore maintain their traditional supervisory role. Separate classrooms meant that pupils could be graded by age and ability. Inside the classroom, work was regulated by the timetable, the clock and the bell. Lighting was sufficiently strong to prevent eye strain and was designed to come from the left-hand side and, as far as possible, from above, to maximize comfortable learning. The room was also organized so that each child was able to see the teacher and the teacher to command the attention of each child. School desks and seats often varied in size and form, but there was a concern to provide as a minimum benches and desks to ensure comfort 'not for sitting at or for standing in – but for both'.[47] The dimensions of the classroom were such that the teacher was able to project their voice for the whole day without any unnecessary effort or fatigue.

Playgrounds in the Board schools remained as important as they were for Wilderspin and Stow. As Robson noted:

'A silent form of teaching': Blackheath High School, London, built 1897; architect E. R. Robson.

The playground is the most important adjunct to a school, and, whether for fresh air, exercise, amusement, recreation or discipline, is quite as necessary in the production of satisfactory educational results as a class-room . . . A good teacher will often be found to regard it as but another place for another kind of instruction.[48]

The ideal playground was one with few 'recesses', so that teacher surveillance could be readily maintained and, like the internal arrangements of the school, it was compact. Part was covered to provide some shelter from wet weather and to provide a space for infants to be drilled, since marching was seen as an important element in their early learning. Girls and infants were divided from the boys, who because of their perceived more active nature required more space. This division usually took the form of a wall, although surveillance considerations led some schools to have

'The uncovered school-room', c. 1874, used to illustrate Robson's *School Architecture*.

railings or, as in schools in Dublin, dividing lines in the playground, which incurred punishment if breached. Play, as with class work, was timetabled and was controlled by the bell or a whistle.

While local traditions, climate and levels of economic development have meant that educational architecture has followed very different courses in different countries, the actual process of building a school followed a general pattern. The local state administration appointed the architect, often after some form of competition, and the publicity given to winning designs in the architectural press stimulated professional interest. The building of the school in line with the architect's plans was then put out to tender. The commissioning body informed all those who had tendered of the name of the successful contractor, who else had bid, and the figures tendered. The successful contractor would then be involved in more detailed inspection of the plans and drawings,

Exercise in the playground, Birmingham, England, 1880s.

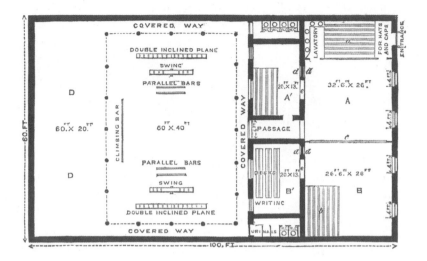

Plan of a playground recommended by the Home and Colonial Society, c. 1874.

preparing the site, erecting site boarding, temporary offices, drains and sheds for workmen and storage, negotiating with local officials and buildings suppliers, providing 'tools, tackle and labour', arranging for insurance during and after building construction (the latter usually including both building and contents), and preparing the new building for occupation (for example, rubbing smooth the slabs of slate for blackboards). There is evidence here and there in building company archives that sometimes the contractors would consult school managers, but this usually concerned minor issues, such as the height of water closets.[49]

The announcement of a new school building in the local press generated a flurry of activity beyond the immediate locality, with manufacturers inundating the contractor and architect with catalogues, quotations and letters of endorsement from satisfied clients as they tried to obtain lucrative contracts for the supply of materials. So, for example, amongst a bundle of papers in the archives of the building firm Sapcote is the following received from Oates and Green, Glazed Bricks of Halifax, Yorkshire, on 22 June 1888: 'We hear you have secured the contract for the New Board School in Sherborne Road, Birmingham. If you require any glazed bricks for this or any other contract you have in mind we shall be pleased to quote you our prices on receipt of particulars of your requirements'. The bundle contains many such 'should you require' letters.[50]

The nineteenth-century school provided work for, amongst others, plasterers, brick and tile makers, tile fixers, plumbers, glazers, painters, excavators, pavers, bricklayers, masons, slate masons, joiners, carpenters, ironmongers, bell founders, roofers, timber and slate merchants, sawmills, iron founders and smiths, locksmiths, steel-bearing manufacturers, gas suppliers and manufacturers of roller blinds, shutters, window cords, water closets, ovens and grates. The contractor received from the architect plans, drawings and specifications. These could include ground and elevation plans, detailed plans of ventilation systems, palisades, play sheds and drains, detailed drawings of roof sections, roof principals, brick-work, dormer windows, joinery for windows, internal and external doors, cloak-horses for a cloakroom, desks and chairs for the master and mistress, cupboards for the master's and mistress's rooms, moveable screens, bell-tower hangings, finger plates, toilets and latrines, classroom cupboards, map cupboards, kitchen cupboards, sills and joints, and detailed specifications for classroom cupboards, travelling desks, map cupboards, step-ladders for book stores, map rods, rubbish boxes for classrooms and playgrounds, towel rollers and letter-boxes. The architect was contracted to check the quality of building materials and to determine the materials to be used – deal for classroom cupboards, travelling desks and platforms; pitch pine for pedestal desks and tables – to sanction any deviation from

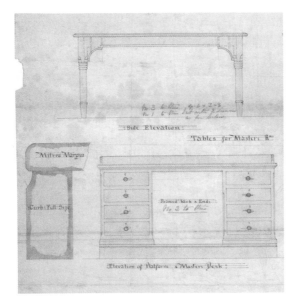

Side Elevation:

Tables for Masters R^m

Mitred Margin

Curb: Full Size.

Framed back & Ends

Elevation of Platform & Masters Desk:

the plans and to dismiss poor workers. In the context of a rapidly expanding national system of education, architects could use plans that had gone before, look and adapt what was offered elsewhere, or develop something new. The imagination of the architect in terms of their design role was, however, limited by site, regulations, economy, efficiency, tradition and knowledge of 'educational matters'. In urban areas land was often so scarce that schools, as Conan Doyle observed, were forced to rise above street level in order to accommodate pupil numbers. Norwood and Hope (1909) found the same phenomenon in both France and Germany:

> schools are much alike in France . . . an average provincial *lycée* will, as a rule, be situated in one of the quieter streets of the town . . . it will rise to the uniform height of four or five stories . . . a school in Prussia

Architect's drawing of desk platform and table side, 1889.

is practically the same as a school of the same type in any other German state [and] as a rule we shall find it . . . rising to the height of four storeys . . . [51]

National and local government building regulations laid down minimum standards relating to the number of square feet or metres of teaching area per child and the number of washbasins and toilets to be provided. Economy and efficiency shaped design possibilities by imposing a ceiling on the cost limit of a school, often calculated per child, and by setting fixed deadlines for completion, which if not met incurred heavy financial penalties. Cost also translated into a desire for the compactness of internal arrangements in a school. Children and teachers moved around the school at different times of the day via entrances, stairwells and corridors, but it was essential that these features should be few in number since they raised costs in terms of ventilation, heating and lighting and required higher staff levels to monitor their use. A lack of compactness in design and excessive movement around a school also meant a continual loss of time during the school day.

The completion of a new school was a major local event, usually involving an official opening, a public meeting, visits by local residents and parents and another report in the press, but the architect's role did not cease at the moment of occupation. Architects were regularly involved in correcting faults to the design in the years immediately after the building was completed. Further, schools were regularly the object of additional work and reconstruction as changing educational ideas or demographic profiles dictated structural additions or minor alterations, and the original architects, if still practising, were commonly involved in this process. Three examples from different parts of Europe can effectively illustrate this point.

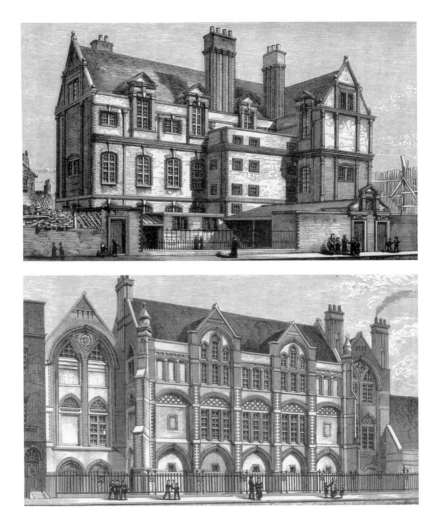

In England, Sherbourne Road Board School, Birmingham, designed by William Hale, was opened in 1889 for 1,618 senior boys, senior girls, junior mixed children and infants. It consisted of two two-storey buildings, built in the Gothic style. The infant

Orange Street Board School, Southwark, London, c. 1872.

Camden Street School, Camden Town, London, c. 1872.

department was closed in 1897. In 1902 a Special School was opened on the site. This had begun as a special class for educationally sub-normal children in 1896 in another nearby Board school. A manual instruction centre was added to the site in 1906. The original school was reorganized in 1930 into three departments for senior boys, junior mixed and infant children. This school closed in 1933 and was turned into a school clinic and youth centre. The Special School continued on site and in the 1950s was renamed Calthorpe Special School; the buildings are no longer extant.

In Sweden, Chapmanskolan is an upper secondary school for 2,400 pupils in the centre of Karlskona. The genealogy of the current school tells a story of building development and continuous reconstruction in response to changing use. The town hall, built in 1750, became a grammar school in 1825. In 1877 neighbouring buildings were purchased from a distillery company to accommodate growing pupil numbers. A Gymnasium school was added in the 1930s. The site was then developed to accommodate first a technical college and then a technical high school. In the 1980s the old technical college was renovated and the old grammar school building was later internally restructured to house spaces for dedicated subject teaching and two assembly halls. Pressure of numbers led to further buildings adjoining the school to be purchased and converted to educational use.

Finally, in Spain, the Instituto Claudio Moyano in Zamora was designed by Miguel Mathet in the early years of the twentieth century. The original design had a quadrangular form around a central courtyard. The school was left largely unchanged until the 1980s, when, because of a lack of large teaching spaces and demographic changes, extensive structural alterations to the existing building were undertaken. The courtyard was covered over to create space for a new entrance hall, a central staircase and a theatre. The floor area of the school was increased by 85 per cent without changing the volume of the building or going beyond its original perimeter. The school now has four floors offering 1,000 pupils compulsory secondary education and vocational training.[52] For each of these schools, every change of use was a stage in the biography of the building.

As the above suggests, it is not unusual to find state schools built in the late nineteenth century still functioning as schools today. In many cases their shape has changed, either enlarged with added structures to encompass more general or specialist space, or reduced in scale as space became redundant. So, for example, in Minden, Westphalia, a school built in the 1890s was used as a grammar school in the 1950s and is now used as a primary school and a special vocational school. Near Hamburg, the 'old town school' at Winsen was also built in the 1890s and is today a primary school. In Hamburg itself, Schule Bundesstrasse, Grundschule Laeiszstrasse, Schule An der Isebek, Max Brauer Gesamtschule and the Helen Lange Gymnasium were all built just before or around 1900.[53] In all these buildings traces of a vanished life remain. These schools are also sites of accumulated pedagogical ideas, practices and materials.[54] Similarly, in North America the one-room nineteenth-century schoolhouse that characterized the first attempt at a state-run, public system of education can still be found – some 400 were functioning as one-room schools in 2000.[55]

In the first half of the nineteenth century schooling took place in a range of locations: in rooms in private houses and buildings, in parts of church buildings, in buildings attached to factories and in large schoolrooms. These sites of learning possessed few external signs that indicated the presence of a school. As industrialization progressed across Europe and North America so too did the

development of state apparatus, and various bureaucratic systems of education were set up to manage a general shift from schooling based on the churches and voluntary enterprise to a system in which the state increasingly controlled the education of the child. Buildings, institutions and employees came together in a process by which the problems associated with organizing mass schooling to meet the needs of advanced capitalist states were addressed through the invention of the public sector. The move towards state schooling stimulated the design and construction of major municipal buildings, which were held as symbols of modernization and urban pride. This was the era that established the practice of employing municipal architects and designers on public building projects. At this time, too, the first school furniture was designed, reflecting a particular interest in the correct alignment of the

An 'old country school', Cowhorn, Kentucky, c. 1912.

Floodgate Street Board School, Birmingham; architects Martin and Chamberlain, opened 1890. The school is now part of South Birmingham College.

child's body, to keep the child alert while sedentary for long periods of time. Schools had existed for centuries, but these new schools were to be 'modern schools' for 'modern times' and 'modern problems'. Their form – characterized by the architectural organization of social space into classrooms, a school hall and playgrounds – was developed from, and in reaction to, existing models, ideas and practices that were in circulation. Their function was to provide basic literacy and numeracy, and in those countries where more than one language coexisted the building of a national identity relied on the learning of a common tongue. Further, it was the politicians, the educational and social reformers and the architects of the second half of the nineteenth century that gave these schools a physical presence and visual identity in the social landscape. The emergence of the 'modern' school also corresponded with the extension across Europe and North America of compulsory education and the diffusion of the Western model of educational systems to settler colonies.

Whatever the local organization, mass schooling institutionalized the separation of children from society. School was a universalized space specifically designed to hold children. It was a space in which teachers developed their professional role, educating and disciplining the young. Control was in the buildings, the space created, and in the material contents of this space – furniture and equipment.[56] Under the influence of school architecture the child was transformed into a *school*child, into a subject of school culture. Children were segregated with their peers according to age and levels of attainment, and sequentially progressed through regulated structures. The school day was structured into timetabled units, and cultural knowledge orientated towards the values and norms of society at large was transmitted. In sum, the school was an instrument of social order, regulating the body and social relations. However, while children were introduced into a school culture, it did not always follow, as the heroine of D. H. Lawrence's *The Rainbow* discovered, that they accepted it:

'If I were you, Miss Brangwen', he said, menacingly, 'I should get a bit tighter hand over my class.'

Ursula shrank.

'Would you?' she asked, sweetly, yet in terror. 'Aren't I strict enough?'

'Because', he repeated, taking no notice of her, 'they'll get you down if you don't tackle 'em pretty quick. They'll pull you down, and worry you . . . You won't be here for another six weeks'.[57]

2 | The School of Tomorrow

> If we put before the mind's eye the ordinary schoolroom, with its rows of ugly desks placed in geometrical order, crowded together so that there shall be as little moving room as possible, desks almost all of the same size, with just space enough to hold books, pencils, and paper, and add a table, some chairs, the bare walls, and possibly a few pictures, we can reconstruct the only educational activity that can possibly go on in such a place. It is all made 'for listening' – because simply studying lessons out of a book is only another kind of listening; it marks the dependency of one mind upon another . . .
>
> John Dewey, American philosopher of education, 1900[1]

If one were asked to identify an iconic school building of the first half of the twentieth century, it would be very easy to single out the 'First Open Air School for Sick Children' in Amsterdam designed by Johannes Duiker and Bernard Bijvoet in 1929–30. The school, which was commissioned by the Association for Open-air Schools for the Healthy Child, expresses the unity between social democratic ideals and architectural modernism. The building is a four-storey cube, almost entirely glazed. Half of each floor opens as a balcony space and the other is enclosed by a glass curtain wall. The glazed rooms had steel-framed revolving windows that could be fully opened. Structural columns were set in the centre of the external walls, giving the balconies a free-floating appearance. Teachers worked with their pupils on the outdoor balconies. The whole effect of the design was that of 'a transparent sparkling crystal'.[2] The design of the Amsterdam school became an inspiration for other European architects who wanted to bring light into schools.

The desire for light realized in the designs of Duiker and Bijvoet and their architect contemporaries was in part stimulated by the emergence of inspection regimes in Europe that monitored the health of children. The efforts of the international 'New Education Fellowship', the influence of the writings of the American educator John Dewey and social and demographic changes also stimulated a review of education systems. There was a sense that public buildings might symbolize a hope for the future and a firm belief that they would not resemble those of the past. The heavy permanence signified by monumental brickwork that characterized the two- or three-storey municipal schools built during the last decades of the nineteenth century would be replaced by a transparent style. 'The demand is for light buildings, with little of the classroom about them, arranged with a view to freedom and variety of use, to possible enlargement and even replacement in the not too distant future.'[3] This sentiment, captured in a poem by Paul Sheerbart, 'Das Glas bringt uns die neue Zeit; Backsteinkultur tutu ns nur leid' ('Glass heralds the future: bricks and mortar, we leave behind'), indicates the optimism associated with new architectural

The Open-air School in Amsterdam, 1929–30: architects Johannes Duiker and Bernard Bijvoet.

possibilities. At the same time, a new openness, flexibility and informality in educational practice began to be advocated by those who were concerned with the failure of education systems to enable the potential of all children to be achieved. The materiality of school would, it was suggested, play a crucial role in enabling new forms of pedagogy to flourish, shifting the centre of gravity from teacher to child. John Dewey recounted his experience of seeking appropriate desks and chairs for the experimental school he founded in Chicago in 1896, when he encountered the following apology from the supplier. 'You want something to enable the child to work and all these are for him to listen'.[4]

As new ideas on hygiene and pedagogy spread across Europe in the first decade of the twentieth century, traditional designs of buildings and furniture were increasingly exposed as failing the health needs of children. This spread of ideas was facilitated by the tradition, established in the late nineteenth century, of national and international pedagogic exhibitions and the study tour. Ventilation in schools was generally found to be poor, the air being unpleasant and likely to cause headaches, drowsiness and irritability amongst both pupils and teachers. A government survey of urban schools in one British city in 1912, for example, found conditions in more than 70 elementary schools unsatisfactory.[5] In Spain, a number of studies and study tours carried out in the 1880s and early 1900s recognized the harmful effects of school furniture, demonstrating that the normal arrangements of desk units that pinned pupils to their places for long periods of time resulted in muscle fatigue, deformations and illnesses, especially short-sightedness and spine curvature.[6] The child-centred educational reformer Maria Montessori carried out a vitriolic critique of the ubiquitous bench-table, suggesting that its use was an outward sign of pedagogic slavery. About the same time in the USA, the birth-control campaigner Margaret Sanger was also calling attention to the inadequate and harmful interiors of schools and kindergartens in the New York district in which she lived. Basement playrooms were

> dark, damp, poorly lighted, poorly ventilated, foul smelling, unclean, and wholly unfit for children for purposes of play . . . The classrooms are poorly lighted, inadequately equipped, and in some cases so small that the desks of pupils and teachers occupy almost all of the floor-space.[7]

Such failings threatened the future of the industrial nations and prompted interventionist actions by governments across Europe to improve the welfare systems available for children, who were seen as investments for tomorrow: 'all children are the natural care of the State . . . We are bound at all costs to see that the children grow up in such a fashion that they may become useful, serviceable and profitable citizens'.[8]

In 1909, shortly after the Liberal Government in Britain had introduced reforms that laid the basis for a child welfare service through schools, Ralph Henry Crowley, MD, was recruited from the pioneering Bradford Education Authority to the Board of Education, where he was appointed Senior Medical Officer in charge of medical staff. Like Robson before him, Crowley believed that the best way to progress the development of school for the masses was through observing the best practices in other countries and continents. Crowley's book, *The Hygiene of School Life*, published the following year, was based on his time in Bradford and has much to say about school buildings, furnishings and organization for teaching and learning. In a section on the school building, he states:

In the planning of the school the aesthetic side should not be forgotten. The keynote should be everywhere simplicity; perfect beauty and perfect hygiene are quite compatible. The school architect should be, of course, as should all architects, an artist: that does not mean that the construction of the school will cost more; a beautiful school, simply built may cost less than an ugly and ornate one . . . the walls should be tinted, preferably a soft grey-green in the more sunny classrooms, and an ochre tint may be used in the less sunny rooms . . . and yellow and red tints should be avoided in rooms naturally bright.[9]

In 1913, as a delegate of the Board of Education, Crowley attended the fourth International Conference on School Hygiene in Buffalo, USA. While on this trip, he took the opportunity to visit several US and Canadian cities to examine progress in medical service provision for schools. In Toronto, he discovered an Open Air Recovery School, established in 1912 on Lake Ontario for 100 children. He visited schools for 'the feeble minded' in New Jersey, and Epileptic Colonies in New York. He became particularly interested in the playgrounds movement that he discovered to be flourishing at this time in some of the major cities on the East Coast. On children's playgrounds, he commented:

there is nothing corresponding in this country to this playground movement in America, although it has been steadily developing there during the past 20 yrs – [where] the school itself becomes the social centre with extensive playgrounds attached [and] . . . the playgrounds form part of the school 'plant'. They are available also for adults . . . and are in continuous use from 7.45 am onwards . . . open all the year round.[10]

In Gary, a new community built around the steel industry in Indiana, Crowley witnessed the practical realization of new ideas about the arrangement of school sites and plants to support the well being and self-directed learning of working-class children. Shortly before his arrival, a progressive educator, William Wirt (1874–1938), had become district supervisor and was best known for his 'platoon' system of alternating two groups of students between classroom and recreational or vocational activities. Crowley visited the Emerson School, where there was 'no classroom, strictly speaking i.e. no one room belongs to any one class', and only a limited number of rooms were fitted with ordinary desks and seats.[11] Particular importance was given to the outside environment and to facilities enabling children to learn practical life skills. Crowley noted: 'Part of the ground is used for school gardens, trees are planted wherever possible, and there are several animal houses constructed by the pupils.'[12] He discovered in the 'platoon' system economy, purpose and popularity:

> The idea of using every part of the school plant as an educational opportunity has been worked out with great success and considerable economy. The upper corridors of the school, for instance, are beautifully lighted and are used as museums and picture gallery.[13]

It was such schools 'without classrooms', where children were motivated by the freedom permitted to them to work at their own pace and at their preferred subjects, and where they could see the immediate usefulness of the work they accomplished, that Crowley chose to highlight on his return in reporting to the Board of Education. Such schools challenged the prevalent rigid traditional structures of education and, for Crowley, showed how real education could be made accessible to ordinary working people.[14]

Crowley's interest and involvement with the United States continued, and in the 1920s he was once again seeking inspiration for his work of developing Child Guidance Services, noting the importance of relating the two areas of education and medicine in the interests of 'the whole child'.[15] A few years later, as his daughter Mary Crowley was beginning her working life as a newly qualified architect, he published *The Whole Child*,[16] which reveals his interest in and knowledge of the experimental village colleges pioneered by Henry Morris in Cambridgeshire. He put the timely question: 'Is it too visionary to see in the school the centre of the educational and recreational life not only of children but also, transcending its present boundaries set by age and type of work, of the community it serves?' His 'intense concern for the mental as well as the physical well being of children'[17] and his socialist leanings led him to develop the concept of 'the whole child' as understood through body, mind and environment. He argued:

> Our study, consequently, must be directed, not to this or that defect, or disease or symptom, but to the whole child – to the body and its physiological working and pathological changes; to the mind, as manifested by the general and specific intelligence and the general and specific behaviour of the child; to the environment at home and at school; to the child's heredity.[18]

The desire for change led to many attempts to capture the nature of the 'school of to-morrow'. The social reformer and educationalist Margaret McMillan did much to draw attention to the importance of fresh air and light for the education of children, stimulating the European-wide interest in the design of open-air schools. Writing in 1919, McMillan issued a plea for a break with the architectural heritage:

> He [a 7-year-old] is going to school? To the big Council School round the corner. It has great walls all round and locked gates and asphalted

playground and stone stairs leading up to big class-rooms . . . The big school is a heritage from yesterday. It has cost a great deal of money, but that does not make it very beautiful, or very suitable, or even efficient . . . It can be changed . . . and it should be changed.

McMillan wanted the 'school of tomorrow' to be 'a garden city of children', where the monstrous 'heavy walls, the terrible gates, the hard playground, the sunless and huge classrooms . . . the awful and grim corridors' would be 'swept away' and children freed from the darkness of the 'prison house'.[19] When Robin Tanner, the influential artist and newly trained educator, first taught in a southeast London elementary school during the 1920s he was horrified by the cramped and uninspiring conditions, 'the children sitting in galleries among walls of shiny privet green and cow colour'. He took the children to visit the Tate Gallery, which, as his biographers noted, was 'an unheard-of innovation'. In his second school, Ivy Lane, Chippenham, Tanner dramatically changed the traditional dull environment by getting the children to paint the school itself. As one School Inspector reported: '[his] classroom had four murals of the seasons on the walls: they weren't complete murals, but rather large pictures, and as I recall they had been executed directly on to the plaster'. Tanner's vision of an educational setting to allow for freedom of movement and largeness of scale helped to inform the educators and architects with whom he later developed close professional and personal ties when he became an Inspector of Schools in Oxfordshire.[20] Beatrice Ensor, one of the leading British activists in the New Education Fellowship, conjured in words in the pages of *The New Era* a future world where education authorities had 'abandoned' all the old, cramped buildings in favour of schools located in the countryside 'so simple in design and so temporary looking; they can always be added to and

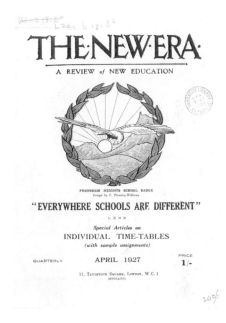

THE·NEW·ERA·

A REVIEW of NEW EDUCATION

"EVERYWHERE SCHOOLS ARE DIFFERENT"

ᴸ ᴴ ᴺ ᴺ

Special Articles on
INDIVIDUAL TIME-TABLES
(with sample assignments)

QUARTERLY   APRIL 1927   PRICE 1/-

11, Tavistock Square, London, W.C. 1
[ENGLAND]

changed easily when necessary'. What was important was 'simplicity, warmth, light, and air, and, of course, beauty'. The schools were the total opposite of what currently existed:

> It was full of air and light and warmth, and there were children everywhere; in the wide verandahs, on the flat roofs, tucked away in quiet corners for study . . . The buildings enclosed a square, grassy court, and were open inside and outside to the sun and air . . . I noticed, too, that windows and doors fitted well, and that the system of ventilation was a good one. Plenty of hot water pipes in the windows, and fireplaces, spoke of warmth and comfort in the winter.

Not all progressive educationalists possessed Ensor's spatial vision, and limited their descriptions of 'new', 'reform' or 'modern'

'Everywhere Schools are Different', in *The New Era*, 1927.

schools to educational practice rather than design. So, for example, in another issue of *The New Era*, Beryl Parker, an American educationalist, reported on her collecting together in 1926 examples of progressive practice in Germany, Austria, the Netherlands, Belgium, France and Switzerland, but made no mention of the nature of school space. Similarly, in the same issue, another American progressive, Joy Elmer Morgan, listed a tentative catalogue of ten characteristics of 'to-morrow's school', but again there is total silence around issues of design.[21]

Much of the interest in the 'school of tomorrow' – McMillan's work being a good example – was focused on the very young and the creation of healthy learning environments for them. Nursery and kindergarten schools were established where light and well-ventilated space connected with progressive ideas about child-centred education – learning through play and the development of the child's personality and identity. The focus on sites of early learning also reflected a greater level of state tolerance towards experimentation, since it was here that 'the clash between a child's development and the nation's requirements . . . [was] muted'.[22] In some contexts this led to the provision of open-air schools, where exposure to sunlight was seen as a means of releasing the vulnerable young from the confines of overcrowded slums and the threat of tuberculosis. In 1907 London County Council built the first open-air school in England at Borstall Wood, while the plan of Letchworth Elementary School (1909), with buildings set around a quadrangle, was influential in its combination of centralization and cross-ventilation. Open-air features were also included in R. G. Kirby's designs for the Buttershaw and Undercliffe elementary schools in Bradford (1908), where there were even baths and showers in the basement.[23] At McMillan's own Open-Air Nursery School in Deptford, south-east London, which was opened in 1914, the children were encouraged to learn outside, resorting to the 'shelters' only in bad weather. Such schools and their perceived success gave architects 'a new task, and new opportunities'.[24]

The calls for change by educational visionaries, however, were also faced with reluctance amongst those who designed schools. The desire to see the educational landscape populated by schools that 'let the sun in' had to compete with a dominant design model of 'a central hall, round which the other rooms are arranged', which was enthusiastically embraced by 'heads of schools [being] unanimous in its favour when once they have tried it', and a model that had met the demands of mass schooling.[25] As the British school architect Philip Robson complained in 1911: 'Architects generally regard schools as the easiest buildings to plan, and much difficulty arises from the fact that architects will not take the trouble to understand the educational side of the case.'[26] Some forty years later, another British architect, Cecil George Stillman, echoed both Robson and McMillan, but also added two other elements to the critique of school architectural practice. 'All too often', he argued, 'a child's first impressions' of school were 'of a bleak expanse of uncompromising tarmac' beyond which loomed 'a flinty Gothic institution' within the walls of which was 'an all-pervading chocolate or green gloom and an almost reptilean dankness'. He continued by stating that education by its very nature was 'constantly changing'; that 'educational theories' demanded suitable buildings; and that for any system to be successful it had to be flexible, but architecture by comparison was 'a static art'. However, he also found both the architect and the educationalist to be at fault: 'the educationalist, for not having fully acquainted the architect with the mutable character of his requirements, and the architect for not having appreciated this for himself and made suitable provision'. Finally, Stillman completed

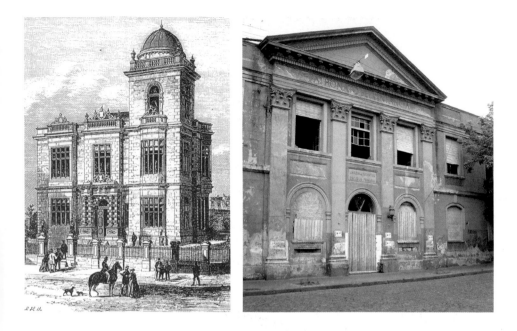

his critique of current practice by drawing attention to the problems that a lack of economic resources posed for new designs.[27] Collectively, these three writers capture the main issues associated with school architecture in the first half of the twentieth century: light rather than darkness; a shift from the memorial design to the functional space; repeated calls for architects to understand the main aims of contemporary educational policy; and the limitations imposed on building programmes by national economies.

Europe in the 1930s was the site of other innovations in school design. Ideas about the connections between health and the environment were circulated and exchanged through national and international social-hygiene exhibitions and congresses.[28] In the north Italian town of Como, the Rationalist architect Giuseppe Terragni, inspired by Duiker's open-air school, used the traditional

South Shields Marine School, 1869; today the building is in use as a public house.

Jardin de Infantes y Escuela Primaria, San Telmo, Buenos Aires; opened 1887, closed 1978.

idea of a *cortile* or monastic cloister to create, between 1934 and 1937, the Asilo Sant'Elia nursery school, a 'glass house for learning'. Terragni's architecture both embraced orthodox modernist positions – 'the new architecture . . . must derive from a strict adherence to logic, to rationality' – and maintained old certainties – 'for us . . . there exists a certain substratum of classicism . . . a spirit of tradition'. The traditionalism that Terragni articulated was deeply imbued with nationalist sentiment.[29] The Asilo Sant'Elia nursery school worked as a dialogue between the inside and the outside, between spaces of meditation and the elements of nature. Open frames, high ceilings and courtyard plans were used to produce a delicate environment of airy, lightly shaded spaces with framed views of greenery beyond. Each classroom had its own outdoor terrace with canvas awnings. Terragni also designed the

Asilo Sant'Elia School, Como, northern Italy 1934–7; architect Guiseppe Terragni, east wing of classrooms, with divisions in bellow stack, allowing for one continuous space, and showing children's furniture designed by Terragni.

chairs, desks, door handles, toilets and other furnishings and fittings inside the building, the lightness and scale of which reflect a deliberate effort to respect the child. Writing in 1975, the architect Reyner Banham described the Asilo Sant'Elia nursery school as the 'best school' built in twentieth-century Italy; it represented 'the most fairy godfatherly compliment ever paid to the young by a modern architect'.[30] The year Asilo Sant'Elia was completed, Kaj Gottlob's School on the Sound in Copenhagen was opened. Like Terragni, Gottlob was also inspired by open-air school designs, notably, the Ecole en Plein Air (1934) in Suresnes, France, by Eugène Beaudouin and Marcel Lods. The Suresnes school was designed to enable children to enjoy as much fresh air as possible, whatever the temperature. On three sides the classroom walls were made of glass panels that could be folded back; classes were also taught outside under the shade of trees or on terraces. Children rested outside or in solariums. Beaudouin and Lods developed a lightweight and essentially rust-proof aluminium alloy to make the school furniture, which even the youngest pupils could carry around. Gottlob's school in Copenhagen was designed around an

The 'School on the Sound', Copenhagen, 1937; architect Kaj Gottlob.

oval atrium that ran the full height of the building, with clerestory lighting entering at the top. The building had four floors, each with a balcony looking down into the main hall, on the floor of which was a large inlaid map of greater Copenhagen. The ceiling was decorated with a great compass rose. This powerful design was combined with a concern for light and the circulation of fresh air to create 'one of the most visionary schools of its era'.[31]

The vision of education that was in circulation in these early decades of the twentieth century was connected with a widespread movement across Europe to 're-make' cities 'in the image of a sun-lit, ordered utopia'. Social reformers, town planners and architects worked together to meet popular demands for better housing, health and education. That said, the alliance between social democracy and architectural modernism to promote the healthy growth and social development of children was often interwoven with other agendas that related to the regulation of the body, notably the new 'science' of eugenics. As Worpole noted, 'every

Ecole en Plein Air at Surêsnes, 1934; architects Eugène Beaudouin and Marcel Lods.

image of the body reformed was ambiguously also accompanied by an image of racial superiority, and even physical triumphalism'.[32] For example, the goals of the French League for Open-Air Education were to:

> contribute, through the development of open-air education, to the restoration of the French race and to the fight against tuberculosis, alcoholism and the causes of degeneracy.
>
> Raise strong and vigorous generations.
>
> Train well developed, active, determined young men and women; men who love their country, are ready to serve and defend it, aware both of their duties and their rights; women who will conscientiously support their husbands, housewives who are attached to their home and prepared for their asocial role.[33]

Worpole was in part echoing the earlier arguments of Roy Lowe, who had claimed a link between movements to establish open-air schools in the English-speaking world with eugenic thinking.[34] Certainly, Western states became increasingly concerned with managing, maintaining and monitoring the health of the popula-

An open-air school in the Netherlands, in an undated photograph.

Open-air school, Birmingham, 1980s: 'inhabited' interior.

tion, and the need for information about a nation's health was accompanied by increased state surveillance.[35] This hunger for information and statistics was seen as a 'healthy hunger'; social reformers hoped for 'the light that may come through figures, and the next few years will give us . . . this illumination'.[36]

In the USA in 1918 all children were required to complete elementary education (8–14 years), but very few working-class children continued beyond this stage. In 1930s progressive American educators used the impact of population growth, migration and urbanization to advance the case for educational reform and were supported by reform-minded Modernist architects, including William Lescaze and Richard Neutra (both of whom had migrated

Open-air school, Birmingham: 'inhabited' exterior, 1950s.

from Europe), who presented their ideas for transforming school design in an array of architectural publications. This was also a period in which stricter child labour laws and the impact of the Depression, at least in the non-Southern United States, pushed up high-school enrolments significantly. Neutra's idea for an 'experimental' school was made manifest in 1935 at Corona Avenue Elementary School in Los Angeles through the construction of an additional set of classrooms in a single-storey building. In order to break the traditional external shell of the classroom so as to facilitate what he termed 'learning through living', sliding glass doors, 12 feet wide, opened onto the school grounds, which, because of the provision of moveable desks, became an exterior work space. Lescaze argued for whole school designs that were sensitive to local demographic and geographic conditions and educational expectations, and he, in turn, was also able to translate these ideas into practice in 1937 with the opening of Ansonia High School, Ansonia, Connecticut. Both schools received widespread publicity, but, as Amy Weisser observes, were 'more promotional than reflective of a new architectural reality'. For many pupils and teachers, the reality of schooling involved attending condemned buildings, learning in deplorable conditions and part-time education because of limited availability of school facilities.[37] Those who did attend new schools – and there were many as a consequence of the government's commitment to public building programmes to stimulate economic recovery during the Depression – found themselves in traditional buildings geared, according to the Boston architect William Greeley, 'to produce a standardized American by the use of . . . standardized desks, in a standardized room with standard air at a standard temperature, under standardized teachers'.[38]

An important, and little noted, contribution to the school building stock across the United States at this time was the initiative spearheaded in 1917 by the Julius Rosenwald Foundation, which financed more than 5,300 schools, shop buildings and teachers' houses built by, and for, African-Americans across the South and Southwest until the programme was discontinued in 1932. Rosenwald, a Jew of German heritage, was president of Sears, Roebuck & Co. from 1908 to 1924. Influenced by Booker T. Washington's autobiography *Up From Slavery* (1901) and dismayed that schooling and much of civic life was segregated along race lines, he wished to improve the opportunities of the black communities and saw the possibilities of overcoming the race divide through schools that were healthy and well designed. Highland Park was one such school built in 1928 in Prince George's County, Maryland. The plans were prepared by the architectural firm of Linthicum and Linthicum of Raleigh, North Carolina, and many local residents worked on the actual construction of the school.[39]

Meanwhile, in Britain, there was much interest in reforming schooling, but an increase in school building during the 1930s ended with the outbreak of the Second World War in 1939 and the refocusing of economic resources. The Haddow Report of 1926, for example, suggested that the education of the younger child required a particular form of pedagogy and associated material environment, reflecting the active nature of learning in the early years. The schools that were built were generally conventional, designed by architects working to detailed standardized written specifications and, as in earlier periods, involved no engagement with those who actually worked inside them.[40] Nevertheless, during the 1930s the British architectural culture did shift towards Modernism. There was a growing interest in a new architecture that responded to human need and used new technology. Scandinavian timber architecture was also influential during this period, and many schools were built of wood, notably Donald Gibson's Hilary Haworth Nursery School at Lache in Cheshire (1935), a timber-framed single-storey building with steel windows.[41] Modernist ideas were disseminated via books, exhibitions, commissions and the physical relocation of architects. Architec-tural developments 'on the Continent' were celebrated in a series of articles in the *Architectural Review*, while the Modernist imperative was advanced with the English publication in 1935 of Walter Gropius's *The New Architecture and the Bauhaus*, and linked to British architectural traditions the following year in Nikolaus Pevsner's *Pioneers of the Modern Movement: From William Morris to Walter Gropius*. An exhibition at the Royal Institute of British Architects (RIBA) in 1937 presented the Modernist school designs of Leurcat, Dudok and Schumacher. Further impetus was provided by the arrival in the 1930s (mainly settling in London) of a number of leading architects – Ernö Goldfinger, Walter Gropius, Berthold Lubetkin and Erich Mendelsohn – who sought refuge from the polit-ical and economic conditions in mainland Europe.[42] Several of the émigrés engaged with school work, but the most significant among the group was Walter Gropius.

The British architect Maxwell Fry, with the designer Jack Pritchard, was instrumental in bringing Gropius out of Hitler's Germany in 1934. Fry later described his role as acting as 'a bogus employment agency' for 'refugees from Germany'.[43] It was Pritchard who, in the same year, introduced Gropius to Henry Morris, Chief Education Officer for Cambridgeshire, a meeting that he described as 'Enlightened architect met enlightened educationist: result: orgasm'.[44] Morris had earlier outlined ambitious plans for the devel-opment of the 'Village College': 'a standard may be set and a great tradition may be begun; in such a synthesis architecture will find a fresh and widespread means of expression'.[45] Gropius confirmed Morris in the opinion of designing 'all contemporary buildings without regard to traditional style', and Morris determined to employ Gropius, as well as Fry, with whom he had entered into partnership, to design Impington Village College. Morris and Pritchard raised the money to pay their fees. Pritchard also persuaded the architect Charles Holden, a friend of Frank Pick, to endorse the project:

> Mr Fry brings to the partnership feeling for the English tradition and a highly developed practical sense, while Professor Gropius possesses one of the most original architectural minds of our time, deeply interested in the social aspect of building and most accomplished using all the results of modern research.

Morris described Gropius's plans for Impington Village College in 1936 as 'superb: a veritable architectural seduction, chaste and severe, but intense' and the following year declared the design 'a masterpiece'. The College opened in 1939 and Pevsner described it as 'one of the best buildings of its date in England, if not the best'.[46]

The College was an elementary school for both boys and girls aged 11 to 14 (aged 15 after the war) during the day, and an adult education and community centre for ten nearby villages in the evenings. The clean and elegant design, built of load-bearing brick, showed how a skilful grouping of the various parts of a building could create a more humane environment, with gardens, trees and playing fields. The school was planned around a central promenade walkway that could also function as an informal social space. An adult wing contained club and seminar rooms.

Such was the impact of Impington on the contemporary imagination that Herbert Read devoted a chapter to it in *Education Through Art* (1943). For him, Impington epitomized a 'practical demonstration of idealism in education' and 'a rallying point for

all reformers who realize the importance of the environment and the functional structure of the school' (from p. viii of the Preface). Not only was it 'practical, functional and beautiful', but it also possessed eleven essential requisites for 'a natural mode of education':

Impington Village College, Cambridgeshire, 1939; architects Walter Gropius and Maxwell Fry.

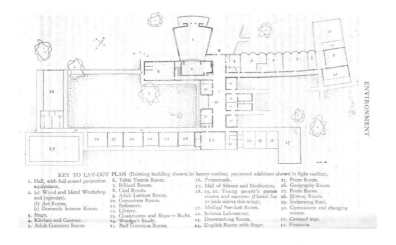

KEY TO LAY-OUT PLAN (Existing building shown in heavy outline; projected additions shown in light outline).

1. Hall, with full sound projection equipment.
2. (a) Wood and Metal Workshop and (upstairs).
   (b) Art Room.
   (c) Domestic Science Room.
3. Stage.
4. Kitchen and Canteen.
5. Adult Common Room.
6. Table Tennis Room.
7. Billiard Room.
8. Card Room.
9. Adult Lecture Room.
10. Committee Room.
11. Refectory.
12. Library.
13. Cloakrooms and Showers Baths.
14. Warden's Study.
15. Staff Common Room.
16. Promenade.
17. Hall of Silence and Meditation.
18, 19, 20. Young people's games rooms and canteens (Hostel for 50 beds above this wing).
21. Medical Services Room.
22. Science Laboratory.
23. Dressmaking Room.
24. English Room with Stage.
25. Form Room.
26. Geography Room.
27. Form Room.
28. History Room.
29. Swimming Pool.
30. Gymnasium and changing rooms.
31. Covered way.
32. Fountain.

Promenade: a large vestibule in which all the personnel of the school – teachers, pupils of all ages and both sexes, can meet and mingle as they come and go, on arrival and before departure, corresponding to the *Peripatos* of Aristotle's Lyceum. *The Theatre*, with stage and full sound projection equipment: with seating capacity for the whole school together with parents and other members of the regional community. *The Withdrawing Room* – a place where the pupil can retire to read or meditate undisturbed.

The various workshops and laboratories [punctuation in quote?]
Work rooms (form rooms and lecture rooms)
Recreation rooms and *gymnasium*
Refreshment rooms (canteens, refectory, etc.)
Library
Services (cloakrooms, kitchen, baths, medical)
External amenities (playgrounds, gardens, playing fields)
External services and *experiments* (vegetable garden, horticultural and stock breeding stations).

Plan of Impington Village College.

The creating of such environments was paramount for Read: 'no services . . . save those nourishing and protecting life itself, should have priority over education'. The question of cost was irrelevant: 'there is land, there are building materials, there is skill and labour'. Read saw no problem in translating the Impington model into urban settings and offered a vision of the future in which cities would have 'one large school in its own park' rather than the current 'five or six schools in back streets'. Such schools would embody 'our new ideals' and their building would be greatly accelerated by the use of 'prefabricated units'. Scale and materials were to be central concerns in post-war discussions about school design.[47]

Writing a year later, Fry reflected on his joint creation and, like Read, stressed the importance of the environment, but in particular related it to the idea of the seamless move between being a pupil and a young adult, using the same site for learning:

> There is no ending, no sudden break. The boy of fifteen working on the lathe, knowing that by autumn his school days will be over, yet sees them continuing full of excitement and hope. Maybe he will go to the farm or to the factory in the village, but for him the college will be as a university, with new stores of experience to be tasted . . . instead of being left in the street or drugged in the cinema, he is there in the college, still growing . . . And this he is doing in surroundings the beauty of which ministers to him unawares . . .[48]

Gropius and Fry also designed a Village School for Papworth in 1937. The project was never realized, although it was published in *Circle: An International Survey of Modern Art*, edited by J. L. Martin, Ben Nicholson and Naum Gabo.[49] Other school designs by émigrés were commissioned in the 1930s, but remained unbuilt. Ernö Goldfinger, for example, accepted a commission from the

Nursery School Association in 1934, which was revised in 1937 and developed for production by Boulton and Paul, but never constructed.[50]

At the end of the 1930s Impington stood boldly for all that was modern and progressive in school building, but the educational landscape was otherwise marked by continuing decay and cries of despair. Delegates to the Conference of Educational Associations of 1937 in London heard Dr Spencer, the former Chief Inspector for Schools to London County Council, argue that 'children [should] be educated according to modern standards, and brought up to be as healthy and vigorous as possible', but he had visited twenty schools in the Midlands and 'fifteen of them . . . ought to be blown up':

> Only one school had a hot water supply, and half of them had no internal water supply. Not half the playgrounds were of asphalt; the rest were of gravel, which turned to mud in wet weather. Not one school had a hall. There were few schools where heating was adequate . . . Children of ten were often too cold to be educated. Scarcely any amenities existed, and five towels a week between 300 children was common.[51]

The education landscape, however, as the Board of Education observed in 1936, was also marked by the presence of a good stock of elementary schools that had been 'built to last a century', a quality that in turn was also seen as problematic in terms of changing educational practice, since these buildings 'were too solid for adaptation without excessive cost'.[52] A similar situation existed in Germany. In a 1960s study of German school architecture, H. Becker observed that any inclination towards educational reform was limited by the existence of a good stock of old school buildings.[53] A small number of these schools, although uninspiring and dull, were transformed by visionary teachers through a strong belief in an educational ideology that emphasized 'learning in an atmosphere of freedom' and the capacity of the school building and outside yard to become part of the curriculum. Thus, Edward F. O'Neill, head teacher at Prestolee School in Lancashire from 1918 to 1951, transformed this all-age state elementary school and, in effect, the school building, its furnishings and outdoor environment became a means through which education was realized.[54] Such ideas were formally sanctioned as an educational philosophy in Scandinavia at this time. In Norway, for example, the primary school curriculum of 1925 was not based on an elaborate school ideology – its scope was confined to prescribing plans for each subject – but by 1939 the national curriculum set out a normative educational approach that demonstrated clear impulses from European and American Progressivism. This school of thought argued for a student-focused school based on the principle of learning by doing.[55]

The outbreak of the Second World War severely curtailed civil building programmes across Europe. In Britain in the early 1940s, the enormous social and civic upheaval of the war stimulated the idea of a national project of reconstruction as a democratic, national project:

> 'New Britain'. I believe those two words are as good a short motto as one can find for all that one wants to do in post-war reconstruction. Most people want something new after the war . . . New Britain sums up the common desires of all of us today, of those who emphasize the New and of those who emphasize the Britain.[56]

The language of reconstruction informed legislation, planning tracts, topographic guides, radio broadcasts, educational manuals and children's books. Wartime books on education and society, trying to create an agenda for post-war change in Britain, also produced a language of community and democracy, sometimes using a liberal elitist adaptation of Christian thought, which appeared to act as the ideological licence for a new educational system and practice. Such ideas were also championed by the range of agencies that focused on the next generation of British citizens. The Council for Education in the Appreciation of Physical Environment, formed in September 1942, for example, used school exhibitions, toys, models and games, lectures and films, teacher-training courses and pamphlets to foster children's awareness of the planned environment.[57]

At the end of the war, in the USA and across Europe, there was both a necessity and a desire to rebuild schools. The Ministry of Defence had commandeered 16,000 schools in Britain, and 5,000 schools had been damaged by bombing. In London alone, of the 1,200 schools in use in 1939, 1,150 had been damaged or demolished by 1945.[58] Money set aside for repairs had been used for the building of air-raid shelters. War damage and lack of maintenance meant that there were insufficient schools to cope with immediate needs, let alone subsequent changes in provision, and at the same time there were severe shortages of money, building materials and labour. Both the USA and Europe also faced a population boom that put further pressure on school-building programmes.[59] In Britain there was a moral panic about war children being out of control and a continuing concern about the health needs of children. In 1947 the Central Council for Health Education in England organized a course for school caretakers that included a session on 'Factors Affecting Health in the School'. The course programme listed the following environmental factors:

Site of School
Type of building, aspect, decoration, canteen accommodation and diet, equipment of all kinds, cloak rooms, drying rooms, showers, lavatories, basins, furniture.
Temperature and humidity of atmosphere.
Fresh air, sunlight, freedom from excessive dust.
General and particular conditions of work exercise, play and rest.
Personal and social relationships of the people in the school.
Standard of cleanliness of premises.[60]

The problem of providing new school buildings was crisis-driven, and the crises kept deepening. The raising of the school leaving age in England from 14 to 15 through the Education Act of 1944 meant that spaces for approximately an additional 400,000 pupils were needed, of which 200,000 needed new school sites. This

An outdoor lesson as a consequence of the requisitioning of a school; the Netherlands during the Second World War.

immediate demand during a period already dealing with enormous repairs to schools required quick and efficient solutions. In late 1943 there had been a conference on post-war building at Aldenham, a village in Hertfordshire, where the architect Stillman insisted on 'the need to use flexible methods of construction, capable of developing with the flow of educational thought rather than buildings which presented teachers with a single solution to their problems which would remain long after they had moved on to new questions'. He emphasized the need for architects to express the evolving ideas of educators rather than perpetuate the static notions of a single moment.[61] The meeting concluded with a number of points about the importance of light materials and community use, and importantly, that a close collaboration between architect and user should be encouraged. Later, Hertfordshire LEA built in whole processes of collaboration between the different professionals needed to organize school building – architect, lawyers, land agents and local administrators. Buildings were to be designed for the children in the first place, then for teachers, and lastly for the governing body. In the meantime, one solution, which immediately addressed the problem of the growth in the school population, was the HORSA hut (Hutting Operation for Raising the School Leaving Age), made of pre-cast concrete.

HORSA huts, built as annexes of existing schools, were described in 1946 as 'a temporary expedient intended to meet a short temporary policy and within a given time'.[62] Between 1 April 1945 and 1 June 1949, 146,445 school places were provided in these huts. Wrotham School in Kent was a typical example. This new school, built by the contractors Dudley Coles in late 1948, consisted of three HORSA blocks on a 10-acre site between Wrotham and Borough Green, together with a small asbestos-clad shed that housed the head teacher and his secretary. The huts were never considered aesthetically pleasing, and at least one local education authority asked if it could avoid taking them. The histories of many British schools included the continuing use of these 'temporary' huts until the end of the twentieth century. The HORSA hut, freezing in winter and sweltering in summer, divided from the remainder of the school, was neither temporary nor mobile, but permanent. The huts came to be much resented, but, as Saint observed, they altered expectations in favour of 'improvisation, simplicity, cheapness and impermanence'.[63]

New ideas circulated during the reconstruction of education in post-war Britain. The pupil was seen as being possessed of a receptive mind, strong curiosity and a fertile imagination. Such ideas did not mean a sudden increase in the number of schools designed for the creative child. Rather, educationalists and policy-makers had to recognize that the school-building programme would impact only on a minority, and that for the foreseeable future the majority of the school population (70 per cent) would continue to be taught in schools built before 1902. It is not surprising, therefore, that one of the most widely distributed publications about post-war schooling sent by the Ministry of Education to every English and Welsh school in 1949 (and again several years later) was a short pamphlet called *The Story of a School*. This told the story of a Victorian-built school in Steward Street, Birmingham, a three-storey building surrounded by factories in a densely inhabited area of the city:

> the school was bounded by factories on three sides. The playground was entirely overlooked by factory windows and nowhere was there the possibility of encouraging a blade of grass to grow. The nearest park was half mile away and there were no open spaces in the near vicinity where children could play in safety.

In a world where pupils had little experience of beauty, A. R. Stone, the head teacher of the school, told the story of how arts education encouraged them to create something beautiful. The lesson was clear. If schools in such challenging circumstances as Steward Street were capable of encouraging children to develop and to be creative, then what school could not? *Story of a School* demonstrated to all its many readers that a school building, dating from the late nineteenth century, with unsuitable wooden floors, poor lighting, a lack of workshop space and heavy school furniture, could also be a 'school of tomorrow' if innovative teaching approaches were adopted. As a result, several educationalists asked

HORSA hut, Mundella Road School, Nottingham, 1951.

The continuing use of huts: a primary school in England, 2000.

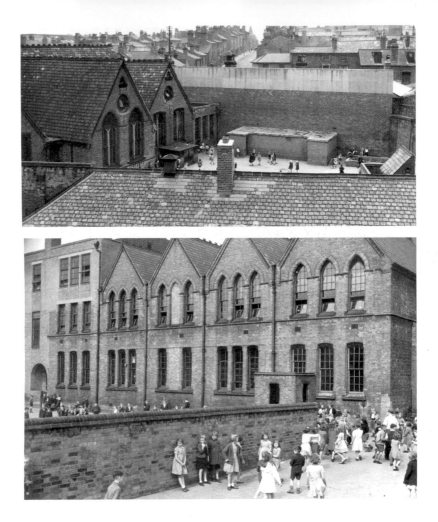

to visit the school, and media interest included an approach to the LEA to make a documentary.[64]

In order to release the child into creativity, the teacher also had to be released. During the war, the difficulties of educating in anything like a normal way had enabled many teachers to experiment, to use environments other than the traditional classroom, and may have led to an increased awareness of the powerful possibilities of

'The school was bounded by factories on three sides': Steward Street School, Birmingham, 1947.

the creative arts in education.[65] The teacher would now have to explain to architects how the new ideas for education would affect the organization of space, learning activities, play and the pedagogy of special subjects. What Stuart Maclure called 'the professional emancipation of the elementary schoolteacher' had to take place before architects could find cultural mediators who would open up this new world of education work:

> The architect is less likely to build the perfect school if he lacks intimate knowledge of the needs of those who will work in it; the teachers will find their work easier in a school in whose design the practising teacher has had some say; and organizers and administrators have all some contribution to make in the planning of a school.[66]

'Story of a School'.

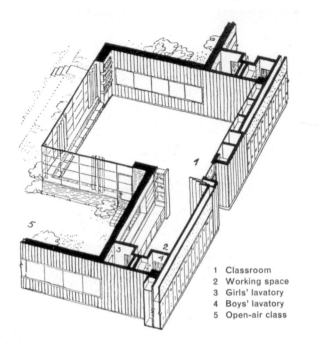

1 Classroom
2 Working space
3 Girls' lavatory
4 Boys' lavatory
5 Open-air class

In the United States, the single-storey Crow Island Elementary School at Winnetka, Illinois, which opened in 1940, was a model for such emancipation. Teachers and other members of the Winnetka school community were all directly involved in developing the single-storey school, as was the School Superintendent of Winnetka city, Carleton Washburne, a passionate advocate of child-centred education who was also president of the Progressive Education Association (1939–43). He was inspired by the laboratory school philosophy and practice that emphasized self-direction in learning and a rejection of classroom recitation. He told the architects, Eliel and Eero Saarinen and Lawrence B. Perkins, that he was looking for 'a beautiful, practical architectural embodiment of an educational philosophy'. They in turn met with both staff and students in order to learn about teaching philosophy and methods. As one teacher wrote to the architect in 1938:

Plan of Crow Island School, 1939–40; architect Lawrence B. Perkins.

Crow Island School.

The building must not be too beautiful, lest it be a place for children to keep and not one for them to use. The materials must be those not easily marred, and permitting of some abuse. The finish and settings must form a harmonious background [to] honest child effort and creation, not one which will make children's work seem crude. Above all the school must be child-like, not what adults think of children . . . It must be warm, personal, and intimate, that it shall be to thousands of children through the years 'my school'.

The resulting school building departed from the traditional Victorian-inspired design so common in the United States, breaking up the monolithic school into a series of smaller units. It consisted of L-shaped self-contained classroom units, each with its own character, all opening directly onto an outside wind-sheltered courtyard or 'open air class'. These were almost like 'isolated cottages' grouped around a central administrative unit, library and auditorium. Large windows and skylights brought natural light into the school. It was also child-scaled, with ceilings several feet lower than usual and light switches positioned at lower heights. Pine-clad walls and linoleum flooring created a warm homely environment. Classroom doors were painted in different primary colours so that children would not get lost. Eero Saarinen and Perkins also designed the school furniture and used natural materials to bring the outdoor world into the school.

Crow Island was a significant landmark in that it offered a model of collaborative endeavour. It was the cumulative result of years of studies carried out by teachers, architects and other technical specialists in common, and it was a model adapted by other similar groupings and networks in the UK. Indeed, Washburne's *A Living Philosophy of Education*, published in 1940, was a major influence on the British architects Mary Crowley and David Medd.

In 1990 Crow Island School was designated a national historic landmark. It has also been twice nominated in architectural journals as one of the most important buildings designed in twentieth-century America.[67]

In England, as hinted earlier, a model way of working emerged in two notable progressive education authorities – ways of working that transformed school building programmes and forged important, long-lasting and influential relationships between educators and architects. In Oxfordshire, where Robin Tanner was Chief Education Officer from 1956, the largely scattered small rural school building stock was to become the source of radical experimentation and innovation in teaching methods. Here, alongside Edith Moorhouse as primary education county adviser, Tanner created a dynamic network of teachers, including David Evans, George Baines (at Brize Norton and later at Eynsham) and Tom John at Tower Hill in Witney, encouraging them to experiment, particularly with creativity and the arts, so that education should be designed around the child. As Evans saw it, 'Slowly, we changed the entire appearance of the classrooms. More than that, we changed our conception of educating children'.[68] The work of Tanner, Moorhouse and, later, Eric Pearson as Tanner's successor as HMI of Oxfordshire paved the way for the open-plan movement of the 1960s.

Hertfordshire, under the educational leadership of John Newsom, also sought the ideal of collaboration between architect and educator. Newsom saw the process as 'thinking about what good primary education might be and how it could be made possible in building', and in 1941 hired Mary Crowley as the first architect to be employed by the county. Hertfordshire worked out that it would need 175 schools, to be built over fifteen years. These schools had to be built as cheaply, simply and quickly as huts, but

Newsom wanted something better. Under the energizing leadership of the deputy county architect, Stirrat Johnson-Marshall, a schools building group was developed that included young architects such as Crowley, David Medd and Bruce Martin. These, together with planners, builders and steel companies, came to develop not a school building but a system of prefabricated school buildings. They used the 'best' or 'imaginative' teacher as the model for good educational practice and designed a building that this teacher could use effectively. Close cooperation between steel makers – who produced girders, struts and window frames – and architects reduced the assembly costs of the light but permanent structures by simplifying the major components, creating a regular system of production based on standardized drawings. The light steel frame units forming the modules could be connected in any direction, thus permitting flexibility in planning.[69] Planners worked with paint manufacturers to produce new colour schemes for rooms and with steel and panel manufacturers to produce structures and cladding. Manufacturers made technical innovations in materials. Crowley designed Burleigh Infants School at Cheshunt, which consisted of just three square prefabricated classrooms, separated by intimate courts for play. Uniquely among architects at the time, she sought out the best teachers, talked to them about their needs and watched children in and out of classes. Such direct knowledge and understanding of the educational process, led by innovative teachers, were then brought to bear on designing schools. From this modest prototype, the whole of Hertfordshire's school-building programme developed. Most of the schools were single- or two-storeyed, but the 100th building of the series, Ravenscroft Secondary Modern School in Barnet (1952), rose to three.[70] A distinctive feature was the range of furniture, specially constructed for schools and incorporating new information about child ergonomics and designed to encourage the new methods of group work.[71]

The resulting schools were praised as representing a fresh approach to planning, as the first major piece of prefabricated unit construction, as a way of building more schools in any given time and as 'important as architecture'. The architects, Richard Llewelyn Davies and J. R. Weekes, captured the essence of the 'Hertfordshire achievement' in an article for *Architectural Review* in 1952:

> It is surprisingly difficult to set down as clearly as possible the general impression that the schools give. It is surprisingly difficult to remember any individual school as a complete building. What remains in the mind is a general impression and individual snapshots, such as a series of passages, the angle of a classroom, an enclosed courtyard. These snapshots are not linked to any individual school, but build up a composite picture of all of them . . . the buildings appear at a distance rather confusing and muddled . . . this contrasts with what is expected from a previous study of the plans. Closer . . . the buildings become progressively more delightful . . . The schools really come to life . . . as one walks round them.
>
> [Once inside] the impression is hard to describe . . . there is a feeling of tremendous exhilaration – a sensation created solely by space, light and colour. The architect trying to analyse the impression he has received feels baffled. Most of the normal elements of architecture are missing. There is no recognisable formal element whatever, proportions seem almost accidental, spaces and planes are divided in the most elementary manner . . . There is an utter and refreshing absence of conscious detailing. There are no materials except glass, steel and plaster.[72]

In the same year, Walter Gropius identified a crisis in the architectural profession, observing that public clients in the United

States were turning their backs on the creative contributions of architects; that the architect was in danger of 'sitting all alone on his anachronistic brick pile, pathetically unaware of the colossal impact of industrialization'. He encouraged American architects to learn from the 'teamwork' in Hertfordshire that had produced 40 new school buildings, each one improving the 'construction, the use value, the price and the beauty' of the building through 'a collaborative effort of a team composed of architects, engineers and builders'.[73]

Schools, especially primary schools, were being designed for new functions and in a new, comprehensive way. These developments were directly connected to the idea of a 'new Britain', one of reconstruction and modernization, and in turn represented a

The 'Hertfordshire achievement': Aboyne Lodge Infants School, 1949–50; architect Donald Barron.

reflection of Modernist visual imagination and concerns with democratic, mass-produced buildings. Several of the architects – Ernö Goldfinger, Carl Franck, Joseph Berger, Peter Moro, Eugene Rosenberg – emigrés from the Continent who had been active in the Modernist movement in the 1930s, were involved in this innovative new phase of school building. Goldfinger, for example, worked on designs for prefabricated schools in London. Greenside School, Hammersmith, and Brandlehow School, Putney (1950–52), both used his own system of concrete prefabrication. These schools were designed to accentuate the scale of a child and were also very cheap to build.[74] Franck, like Goldfinger, also worked on designs for prefabricated schools. Berger designed Woodberry Down School (1946–50) for London County Council

Ernö Goldfinger's infant school at Putney, south-west London, 1950–52.

(LCC). At the time – and can still be regarded as such – it was viewed as a pioneering project because he insisted on consulting teachers about what they wanted, much to the dismay of LCC administrators, who feared both additional costs and delay. The school is designed as a square, with three four-storey teaching blocks, each with blue-tiled curved tops to the stairwells and two assembly halls with wavy rooflines on the fourth side.[75] Rosenberg designed the Susan Lawrence Primary School in Lansbury (1950–51), which used a factory-produced steel frame manufactured by Hills Ltd, the use of which kept down site labour costs. The school has an infant's department on the ground floor and a first-floor junior department. The two departments had a shared dining room and entrance hall, the latter featuring decorative tiles by the artist and teacher Peggy Angus. The tiny Elizabeth Lansbury Nursery School was built alongside the school, and both designs were featured in the borough's Town Planning Exhibition at the Festival of Britain. Rosenberg also worked on

Infant school, Putney.

Dick Sheppard School, Tulse Hill, Brixton (1950–56), which was designed as a school for 960 girls, but became a mixed comprehensive school. The school was conceived as a campus of eight classroom blocks overlooking a nearby park. A concrete portal gives shape to the large entrance and assembly hall. As with the other designs by this group of architects, there is decorative art in the form of a large mural.[76] Finally, Moro also received commissions from the LCC and designed Fairlawn Primary School, Forest Hill (1955–8). His design consisted of three units: an assembly hall/dining room; a curtain-walled block of junior classrooms built around staircases so that the classrooms are glazed on both sides; and a single-storey infants' block, linked by offices and entrance.

Towards the end of this period of educational reconstruction, the American architect and photographer G. E. Kidder Smith noted in his book on the new architecture in Europe – a text that in many ways parallels Robson's of a century earlier – that 'the English achievement in building schools is recognized everywhere'.[77] He presented detailed descriptions of several English schools. Richmond High School for Girls in Yorkshire was completed in 1940. A young architect, Denis Clarke Hall, was commissioned by Frank Barraclough, a progressive education officer in Yorkshire, to design the school after winning a competition sponsored by the *News Chronicle*. His design was one of elegant modernity, using both the natural landscape and local stone. The building consists of a simple block, with all of the classrooms on the top floor, along with the library. The classrooms, with glazing on one side set into concrete frames, are isolated in pairs. They are connected by separate passageways to a wide central corridor, which functions as the spine of the building.

Hunstanton Secondary School in Norfolk, which opened in 1954, was also designed by young architects: Alison and Peter

Smithson. Winning a competition in 1949, the Smithsons, who had been clearly influenced by Mies van der Rohe's work in Illinois, were determined to produce a formal and compact two-storey main block, with all the noisy activities of the 510 pupils located in one-storey adjuncts. The plan was almost symmetrical, with the buildings organized around two courtyards, set on either side of the school hall. The administrative and group activities were all placed on the ground floor, and the classrooms were grouped in pairs on the second floor, access to which was from ten small staircases. There were almost no corridors, and pupils circulated by way of the entrance lobbies and the large two-storey assembly hall. The lack of corridors meant that each classroom could be glazed from floor to ceiling on both its north and south sides, and the use of steel frames without subframes maximized the effect, although led to heat loss. Such transparency provided a maximum of controllable natural light, which for Kidder Smith was the building's strongest feature. The services were exposed to view, almost creating a decorative feature.[78]

On its opening the first head teacher of the school told the educational press that staff and pupils alike appreciated the new

Richmond High School for Girls, Yorkshire, 1940; architect Denis Clarke Hall.

building's design. The chief education officer for Norfolk was a little more cautious, stating that the ultimate success of the school would depend on whether the teachers could 'establish a school in a building so transparent', because 'they must secure the attention of their children in a market wide open to potentially competing interest'. He added that 'nothing can change the fundamental conviction that the educational function of a school must take precedence over any theory of aesthetics'.[79] Some commentators in the architectural press were openly hostile, with one critic observing under the leader 'The New Brutalism':

The Smithsons: Hunstanton Secondary Modern School, Norfolk, 1954 (now Smithdon County High School).

Architects should walk into the assembly hall and classrooms and see for themselves the gault brick walls, the exposed RSJs, the exposed rough pre-cast concrete floor painted white, the troughed asbestos ceiling in the assembly hall . . . the exposed pipes and conduits . . . There is not one single piece of soft material anywhere in the building. It will be interesting to know the noise level when it is full of children . . . Indeed . . . this building seems often to ignore the children for which it was built . . . it is a formalist structure which will please only the architects, and a small coterie concerned more with satisfying their personal design sense than with achieving a humanist, functional architecture.[80]

Others celebrated the school's potent style. Kidder Smith described Hunstanton as 'one of the great new schools in England', which 'exerted a strong influence on subsequent work'.[81] Certainly, the boldness of the design appealed to the next generation of British

Classrooms and stairway at Hunstanton.

architects, but it was the only English state school designed by the Smithsons and there is no evidence that the design had a serious influence on later school building.

Another secondary school, Churchfields School in West Bromwich, designed by Richard Sheppard and Associates, was singled out by Kidder Smith as a 'splendid solution' to the 'problem' of the large school. Opened in 1964, the school, constructed of concrete, steel and wood, consists of a group of twelve 'houses' or mini-schools gathered around a central core of interconnected libraries, work-shops, offices and assembly halls. Each house is designed as a learning and social base for the children, containing individual classrooms on two storeys and a space for meals and other com-munal activities. It accommodated between 180 to 360 pupils. Sheppard's design is very much in the mould of McMillan's idea of separate school communities in a garden city of children, but on a much larger scale. It also reflects his ideas about community space, which he developed in his earlier design for the Village School at Little Wymondley, Hertfordshire.[82] A very different design both in scale and execution is Bousfield Primary School, London, by Chamberlin, Powell and Bon, which Kidder Smith described as 'among the finest primary schools yet designed' and 'one of the best schools in Europe'. It was built on the site of several bombed houses and used subtle changes of level to accommodate more than 500 infant and junior-aged pupils. Two large assembly halls, constructed back to back, are at the centre of the design, separated by enclosed courts from the two sets of classrooms. To complement the enclosed structures, the design uses gardens, including a water garden, to create 'sensitive spaces'.[83]

Kidder Smith also listed an additional seventeen 'English schools of distinction'. These included work by both Moro (Fairlawn Primary) and Rosenberg (Susan Lawrence School, Stevenage New Town Secondary School). While singling out the quality of English school design for praise, he was at the same time critical. English classrooms, he wrote, 'were generally overcrowded, often in excess of forty pupils, many schools were consequently far too large, with over 2000 pupils, and too few of schools had any art'.[84]

Across the rest of Europe, Kidder Smith's case-study gazetteer of iconic modern school architecture was limited to three schools in both Denmark and Switzerland, and one each in Germany and Sweden.

Kidder Smith's selection represented 'the cream' of post-war architecture in Europe. A word of caution is necessary here, however, especially if the focus is the English schools. In subsequent surveys of English school building – Seaborne and Lowe (1977), Saint (1987), Dudek (2000) – Churchfields and Bousfield do not feature at all, while criticisms of the Smithsons' design are uniformly voiced. Dudek, in particular, presented evidence of the failings of what he termed the 'infamous' Hunstanton School, notably that the design made it almost impossible to extend and, citing the current head teacher, that the building did not work for its inhabitants: 'a bit of a nightmare because the building is too cold in winter, hot in summer, the interior is too noisy and open and creates teaching difficulties, maintenance costs are high'.[85] Richmond is the only design where these later writers are in agreement with Kidder Smith. Dudek praised Richmond as 'a spirited building', incorporating new spatial relationships that expressed a raw modernism, and speculated that it must have been an inspiring building for children to grow up in during its early years. Indeed, Sir James Richards in his *Introduction to Modern Architecture* went as far as to describe Clarke Hall's Richmond design as 'the first example of modern school building in England'. However, he also noted the subsequent criticisms that it was a building that treated education as a process and showed little concern for the needs of those who were taught and worked in its spaces. Like Hunstanton it was too cold in winter, too hot in summer and too noisy. Worse still, it became a model design that was 'plagiarised in less appropriate settings by less accomplished designers'.[86]

Looking back over the first half of the twentieth century, it is clear that darkness was ignorance, and light civilization. Schools, as Lawn noted, 'were to be light in construction, the school transparent, the classrooms illuminated, and the pupil and teacher enlightened'.[87] Light, as we have seen, did enter education, but at the end of the 1950s the reality of school life for many pupils and teachers was that the 'school of tomorrow' remained just that, a dream and a promise. To take just primary schools in England and Wales, a school building survey of 1962 identified that 44 per cent of pupils were being taught in buildings erected before 1902. The survey also showed that 66 per cent of primary schools had out-door toilets; 26 per cent had no warm-water supply for pupils; 25 per cent had no central heating system; and 40 per cent were classed as being of a sub-standard site – having less than two-thirds of the area prescribed as necessary by the School Building Regulations of 1959.[88] Furthermore, as Seaborne observed and demonstrated in 1971 with regard to primary-school design in England, 'the "show" school of one generation easily became the "slum" school of the next'.[89]

New designs, for example, the open-plan primary school, which began to emerge in the 1950s as architects moved to reduce cir-culation space, connected with a desire amongst some education-alists and policy-makers to be more responsive in design terms to the differential rate of a child's physical and emotional develop-ment. There was also a pedagogical shift to encourage teachers to use both space and ancillary staff more effectively, and a concern to foster greater parental involvement in school life. Such new designs, however, did not always sit comfortably with teachers who, having spent large parts of their careers working in tradi-tionally designed classrooms and employing traditional methods and resources, were re-housed in new learning spaces designed for new ways of working.

Teachers still remained largely silent partners in educational design. An interesting exception was reported in *Education* in 1954, when the head teachers of several new schools were given a post-occupancy opportunity to comment on 'The Teaching Aspect'. One school, Howardian High School for Boys in Cardiff, had been designed by a former pupil, Sir Percy Thomas, and while the head teacher praised the quality of the light and the ventilation, and described the specialist facilities as 'leaving nothing to be desired', the bulk of his commentary related to the teaching problems created by the design. Communication was a problem because departments were 'widely distributed'. The design isolated some parts of the school, which because there was no internal telephone system made 'efficient control and supervision very hard'. There was also a shortage of classrooms, which meant that specialist rooms lost 'their individuality and much of their value' when they had to be used for a dual purpose. While contour planning of buildings led to economies of cost, 'steps and stairs in and outside the building increase the potential dangers', and rendered supervision and control again difficult.[90]

Finally, a continuing thread running through this period was the recognition, though rarely acted upon, that the fixtures and fittings designed to go inside a school impacted as much upon the child, the teacher and the administrator as the corridor arteries and other structural features that shaped the daily rhythm of school lives. A report of 1937 cited evidence from the National Union of Teachers that 'bright, harmonious [colour] schemes' in schools in Geneva, Copenhagen, Lausanne, Rotterdam, Lyons and Stockholm stimulated children 'to appreciate colour and cleanliness' and 'provide[d] happier surroundings for school work'.[91] English school furniture and equipment were found to be 'too much dominated by convention' and lagging 'behind school architecture though the two ought obviously to keep step'. There was 'no better way of teaching design' than by making the 'actual school an object lesson; it should be well planned, not only in its general design, but in all the details of the furniture, equipment and material brought into it'. McMillan, Read, Pritchard and Morris all pointed to the need to consider the materiality of a school building if it was to be an efficient working tool of education. For Morris, the efficiency of a building depended upon knowledge of the 'materials, lighting, storage, orientation, heating, corridors, equipment, styles of tables, desks, seats, etc., having in mind . . . the pupil and the experiences of the teacher', while for Read, 'the furniture and fittings of a school should properly be a part of the architect's function . . . Many a good school is spoilt by hideous desks or inappropriate lighting'.[92] Such concerns were seized on by some architects – Terragni in Como, the Saarinens and Perkins in Winnetka, the Medds in Hertfordshire – but they remained the exceptions.

3 The 'Expanding School' and the 'Exploding Classroom'

The child is the unit around whom the school revolves.[1]

Between the immediate post-war years and the 1960s, most states in Europe were intent on the renewal and reconstruction of their public services. New opportunities and challenges faced the modern democracies that had survived the war, and some regions saw the renewal of educational environments as a means by which democracies might be rebuilt or strengthened. Nation states such as Denmark, Norway, Sweden and Britain chose to strengthen their social democratic infrastructures and invest in social welfare and public education. In France, public secondary education had become entirely free in 1934, but it was not until after the war that the *lycées* became schools for the masses and not just the elite. Some post-Fascist states such as Italy began to recognize in the reconstruction of education for young children the possibilities of building democracy and a resistance to Fascism in the long term. A unique approach to pre-school education was introduced in Reggio Emilia, in northern Italy, designed by educators and parents, and inspired by the visionary founding director, Loris Malaguzzi (1920–1994). This pre-school educational ideology recognized the child and adult as first and second 'teachers' and emphasized the role of the building, its interiors, textures, colours and dynamics, as 'the third teacher'. Such school environments for the very young would signify and support the social value of education in a society committed to critical thinking as a foundation for a strong democracy. In a spirit of renewal provoked by the destruction of war, other educators and architects during these years envisaged the building of a school as a 'third teacher'. In its very design and organizational layout, this should speak of a democratic and egalitarian society, where individuals were respected and their capacities as young citizens acknowledged. Kindergartens, primary schools, community schools and colleges were viewed as sites where the inequalities of society might be countered.

For the younger child, educational environments that emphasized flexibility, learning through doing and a pedagogy that supported self-directed learning rather than instruction were envisaged. Some considered that such pedagogy was necessary to build a society equipped to resist political indoctrination. For the older child, most post-war democracies gradually came to see the idea of the 'comprehensive school' as the preferred tool for nation-building at a time when nationalism itself had become seriously blemished. Comprehensive education, it was thought, required the kind of architecture that enhanced and embraced social community, where children were evidently welcomed to be educated together, regardless of their social or educational backgrounds, 'ability' and 'aptitudes'.

An international survey of schools conducted in the late 1960s and early 1970s, whose buildings were thought to be 'representative of advanced pedagogical thinking, was published in 1975.[2] Operational flexibility, shared community access to facilities and the exploitation of new technologies and materials were common features of the schools selected. Brooks Road Junior School in Toronto, Canada, was described as a 'very pure example of open-plan as understood in North America'.[3]

Following the Education Act of 1944, secondary education in England was initially organized on selective lines, although Local Educational Authorities were permitted to adopt the comprehensive (non-selective) system if they felt it was appropriate to their needs. But the building stock was limited, as were funds, and this led most LEAs to adopt the 'tripartite system', referring to the three types of children it was believed could be identified through intelligence testing at or around the age of 11, and to provide schools accordingly. For most English children, there were two types, grammar and modern, while Wales and Scotland chose to organize a comprehensive system from this time. The resulting post-war, free, state-supported English grammar schools were established in some of the oldest school buildings, which for many years previously had largely served the children of the wealthy middle classes.

Comprehensive schools were therefore relatively uncommon during the 1940s and '50s, but those that existed were intent on signalling their difference from the norm. In England, their rise coincided with a national commitment to financing new schools, which in turn produced buildings that used experimental and innovative building materials and engineering techniques. Some comprehensive schools and community colleges in progressive local authorities such as Leicestershire were built to designs that emphasized community, inclusion and social learning, and these will be discussed below. The discourse of the time, for schooling at all levels, emphasized a break with the past and projected the vision of a new dynamic relationship between school, community and wider society. School buildings that 'fused' with or 'exploded into' the community were imagined for older children, while 'the expanding classroom' was a motif for the primary school.[4] Boundaries would disappear as school became community, while community would become school.[5]

In post-war Germany, the architect Hans Scharoun experimented with ideas of appropriate design for a school in keeping with contemporary cross-national concerns to deliver child-centred education and to strengthen the democratic society. It is worth considering Scharoun's work in some detail since it illustrates in microcosm what were more generally held beliefs and approaches among innovative designers and educators during these years, some of which will be discussed further in this chapter in other national contexts. Scharoun was born in Bremen in north-west Germany in 1893 and grew up in Bremerhaven. In his youth he became associated with the Utopian architects grouped around Bruno Taut in Berlin, also known as the Expressionists. In his early work, an appreciation of the human at the centre of architectural design was already evident. He stated: 'The human being should be at the centre, with our aspirations forming a lofty vault over us like the firmament.'[6] Scharoun's school architecture began in the

Model of Darmstadt school plan, 1951; architect Hans Scharoun.

early 1950s, a crucial event in 1951 being the conference *Mensch und Raum* ('Man and Space') held in Darmstadt. This event brought together architects, sociologists and philosophers, including Martin Heidegger. Prior to the conference, ten architects were invited to bring designs for public buildings. Scharoun presented his ideas for a primary school, which, although never built, is thought to be significant in changing the ways that architects thought about designs for schooling.

For Scharoun, it was important to develop an architectural approach that would be experienced by children as a warm, lively and emotionally nurturing environment through which they might come to the knowledge of individual identity and community belonging. This involved a rejection of the cold, institutional arrangements of the traditional school. In this sense, his work offered the realization of what was thought to be vital but difficult to achieve in the design of a learning environment for the developing child.

A crucial feature of the design was the idea of the form of the classroom, or 'class-dwelling', as matching or mirroring an idea of the child at its stage of development as an individual. What was important for Scharoun was the idea that the school building design would symbolize and thus nurture the child as it developed from its domestic and intimate nest-like beginnings in life towards a more outward-looking attitude, ready to connect with the community and the wider world. The challenge was to achieve a design that would act as a second home and develop independence of spirit and personal responsibility. In the post-Fascist era, such an aspiration became a political priority in order to challenge the authoritarianism of the past and the passivity of the young. The 'public' areas of the school where social interaction might happen, whether formal or informal, were considered to be as important as the spaces for formal learning. With flattened hexagonal shapes for classrooms and polygonal shapes for assembly areas, the architecture encouraged a circularity, with furnishings arranged in a democratic form appropriate for discussion and active participation in learning. The architectural historian Peter Blundell Jones has likened Scharoun's schools to small cities, made up of a series of spaces in relationships.[7]

The Geschwister-Scholl-Gesamtschule (School for Girls) in Lünen, North Rhine-Westphalia, brought into fruition many of the ideas that Scharoun conceived in the early 1950s, although it was actually built between 1956 and 1962 as a grammar school for girls from the ages of 10 to 18. As Blundell Jones put it, 'The school was planned like a small city, as a series of articulated parts linked by an irregular internal street, a world with clearly perceptible spatial hierarchies.'[8] The form of the rooms took account of the nature of the activities that would take place in them and the ages of the pupils. One group of rooms comprised the *Klassenwohnung* (literally 'classroom-flat', which means that a single classroom consists of main teaching space, teaching annexe, entrance lobby and outdoor teaching area) of the lower-, middle- and upper-grade pupils, conceptualized in different ways according to age. The rooms were designed to emphasize the different stages of an individual's development by the use of colour and light. The rooms for the youngest thus took on the character of a nest, while the middle groups were characterized by exactness, and the higher ones by the peculiar phase of development between childhood and adult. This latter phase was shown by the upper classrooms on the first floor looking out on the outside world. The areas with a more individual and almost private character were connected with the other parts of the school by a street-like flowing internal space also used as a break-hall. Thus the connection of the individual to the community

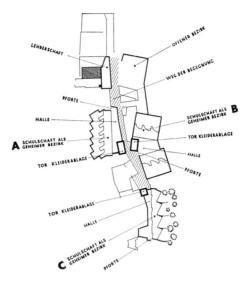

was not only symbolized but also effected in the everyday life of the school. The layout resulted in a complex of apartment-like classrooms, built to create for the pupils a continuous link between the home and school environments.[9]

The rooms were shaped like pavilions (flattened hexagons, to accommodate both linear and circular seating layouts), avoiding right angles. Each of these 'dwellings' consisted of a teaching area, an entrance space extending the main classroom area with wash-hand basins and coat hooks, a main classroom, an added bay where a small group could work separately and an area for teaching in the open air. Although the class dwellings for each of the three age groups consisted of the same elements, they differed in the relations between the inner and the outer areas. These varying degrees of openness rested on Scharoun's understanding of the different levels of the girls' development, drawn presumably from

Plan of the school for girls in Lünen, North Rhine-Westphalia, 1962; architect Hans Scharoun.

his conversations with medical and educational experts at the time. This was emphasized through the lighting – daylight is spread evenly around the rooms from small windows underneath the ceiling – and the different heights of the rooms. The general communal spaces of the school were given a public character by means of drinking fountains, benches, notice boards, showcases, plants and a milk bar. Walls were generally plastered and painted, with timber joinery and some exposed concrete columns.

The plan of the school at Lünen shows the correspondence of relatively small and shielded class apartments to spacious and generous public rooms. The rooms are very differentiated and their purpose is very legible from the plan, at a time when most schools followed a dull uniformity set by the construction grid. In Scharoun's opinion, this extraversion and introversion, the relationship of inside and outside space, of openness and unity, formed the essence of a school. His pursuit of the ideals of organic architecture led Scharoun to build a school based on his interpretation of the child's point of view. The worlds of teachers and children were both considered here, but the priority in design terms was given to the world of the child: no longer cold and distant but warm and appropriate to their stage of development as a human being in the world. Thus the staff rooms were located at the perimeter of the building. Scharoun was not particularly interested in rationalizing time and space for the purpose of teaching. Instead, he attempted to build a school that would support children's learning and development as social beings, taking into account their needs as he understood them. Children's attachment to the space they occupied and their feeling of well-being and identification were more relevant to Scharoun than organizational and technological efficiency.

The completed school was praised for its polygonal forms, which were perceived as a liberation from formal obligations and inflexibility. Scharoun's ideas for school buildings, however, met with little response. They did not respond to public demand for simpler and cheaper solutions, for rationalized and fixed types that would facilitate the series production of school buildings, which became a crucial item on the agenda following the enormous growth in the number of pupils and economic shortfalls after the Second World World War. It was also felt that, in the end, in its intention of regulating behaviour and the relationship between pupils and teachers, Scharoun's subjective architecture ran counter to his democratic intentions.

Experimental and innovative designs such as the school in Lünen were inspirational, and did speak of the importance of wedding individual identity with belonging and community, within settings that provided a domestic or home-like ambience. We will see below how elsewhere pioneering school architecture and associated pedagogy embraced such an emphasis during these years. However, the need to build quickly, efficiently and cheaply in order to meet the demands of reconstruction and the rising birth rate was felt as a pressing priority by most Western nation states. Efficiency and speed of construction through the innovative use of newly available building materials and engineering possibilities ran alongside a renewed interest in the needs of the developing child and the design of appropriate and fitting pedagogy. Indeed, whether the school was designed for the very young or the adolescent, understanding the developing child in its environment was considered seriously.

Hope was built into school design and confidence too that the particular arrangement of materials in designed spaces would encourage positive self-awareness and would help to develop and cement cooperation between groups of learners and teachers. There was considerable confidence that design could enable children to

exercise more choice in learning; confidence that they would move freely and purposefully from one activity to the next, supported and scaffolded by a wise mentor – a teacher or group of teachers. There was hope that the subdivision of children and the curriculum would be overcome as a more thematic approach to learning enabled all children to learn across the disciplines, the younger learning from their older peers in vertical groupings. Through practice, it was realized that teachers could, if supported, prescribe the environment of the school, release the children permissively into it, observe their activities to diagnose their needs, and draw upon their professional resources to meet those needs. And there was optimism that the new educational arrangements, including education for the very young child, would help to create social justice and prevent world conflict, ensuring peace and reconciliation in an era that still bore the scars of war.[10]

Walls and doors were regarded as metaphorical as well as physical barriers to the potential flow and connectivity believed to be

Children at Eynsham Primary School, Oxfordshire, 1965.

crucial to the learning experience. In this sense, material conditions had to mirror pedagogical intentions. Some progressive educationists thus thought that architects should be designing for an ever increasing variety of interconnected activities, readily available to groups of children and their teachers for the exploration of problems they set themselves. The removal of the familiar barriers and boundaries that had traditionally separated children from their teachers at school was a sign that this was achievable, at least for the education of the younger child. This included the abolition of the division between the infant and the older child in primary schools and the design of schools without doors, 'as these stop the flow of ideas from imaginative people who initiate them or from gifted children who develop or extend them'.[11]

There were signs, during these years, of a retreat from the extremes of Modernism and a shift towards an architectural humanism characterized by an interest in the behaviours, feelings and aspirations of the people inhabiting the buildings. This encouraged an attempt to view the interior of the school from what were considered to be the two principal viewpoints, of child and teacher, which contrasted sharply. The world of the teacher – of freedom of movement and, at that time, considerable freedom in interpreting the curriculum and in adopting ways and means of disciplining children – contrasted with the world of the pupil – a rigid one of restrictions, rules and regulations. This 'colder' world was captured in images of the secondary school in popular culture. One example was the noted film documentary 'High School' by Fred Wiseman, screened in 1968, in which North East High, Philadelphia, a large school for approximately 4,000 all-white children, revealed its cold, harsh corridors and classrooms. Cited by the Library of Congress as a National Treasure, this film is both a document of the times and a reminder of the constancy of school cultures over time and place.

An effort to lower the adult gaze to correspond to that of the child, literally to see the world from the pupil's point of view, is noticeable in popular educational literature of the time, some of which inspired a generation of teachers then entering the profession. Many student teachers referred to Edward Blishen's *The School That I'd Like*, published in the UK in 1969, which contained powerful statements by secondary school children about their experiences and their hopes and dreams for a better education. The American educationalist John Holt was also popular. Writing in the 1970s and published in the UK, he reminded his readers that children were naturally sensitive to space and that the designed and built environment was a significant factor in their educational journeys.[12] Holt's works, including *How Children Learn* and *Why Children Fail*, encouraged those interested or engaged in education to look at the school through the eyes of the young child, picking out the spaces, places, textures and smells that held meaning for them, but which were forgotten or lost to the adult.

The post-war years were also characterized by a review of schooling for children that had particular requirements. Until this time, children with physical or mental impairments generally attended special schools and were separated from other children in their communities and even from other members of their families. In Britain, Baroness Warnock, who chaired an inquiry into the education of 'handicapped' children in the 1970s, argued in her review that all children should have the right to a place in a mainstream classroom. This placed an enormous challenge to existing schools, which had been designed with the 'normal' child in mind. Limitations on capital spending in the UK following the oil crisis of 1973 meant that it would be many years before schools could be redesigned and built to support inclusion. The health and wellbeing of all schoolchildren continued to be a concern, but interest in open-air schools lessened when antibiotics were introduced as a cure for tuberculosis after the war.

Getting down to the level of the child, seeing that world through the child's eyes and imagining their experience were means by which architects could argue the case for a new approach to architecture, which celebrated its social and liberatory capacities. Some architects began to ask children what they wanted their schools to look and feel like, and thought the answers worth consideration. In an article entitled 'The Children Want Classrooms Alive with Chaos', Barbara Villet, writing in the USA, presented the newly built English primary schools as an inspiration to contemporary American architects and teachers. She presented in her feature a list of ideas offered by children between the ages of 5 and 12 to the Boston-based school architect Walter Hill. The list included the following demands, which suggest a need to design for learning in an atmosphere of freedom:

'Put the desks in the halls so we can use the rooms'
'We need a clothes dryer and cabinets with messy paint and shoe polish'
'Make it so we can walk around because we were born free'
'A rocking horse to sit on when you need to think and a bed to read in'
'It has a sign on everything that says PLEASE TOUCH'
'A mouse in school would make it better and can I bring my jar of ants?'[13]

There were other architects interested in seeing the school from the point of view of the innovative teacher, in order to design new learning environments that would overcome the limitations posed by the buildings. The ideals of progressive education did have proponents in the United States (John Dewey's laboratory school in Chicago, founded in 1906, was an early example of these ideas in practice), but Cold War anxiety and cultural conservatism during the 1950s led to their wide repudiation by the establishment. For the moment, progressive education disintegrated in the USA as an identifiable movement. Things were very different in Britain, where a new generation of architects and educators, many of whom had been educated in independent progressive schools, had been brought together through the unique circumstances of the war years. They created a particular dynamism in their work, so much so that international attention was drawn towards their achievements.

Having pioneered the design of infant schools while working under Stirrat Johnson-Marshall during the 1940s and '50s in Hertfordshire, the architects Mary Crowley (later, Medd) and David Medd had become crucial players in the Research and Development Team at the Ministry of Education, working with county councils in creating design prototypes for schools around the country. The architectural historian Andrew Saint has commented on the relatively unique status of the English primary school: 'the child-centred, activity-oriented approach to primary education which inspired the school-building movement at Hertfordshire never found such a firm support in national policy elsewhere [and] the architectural and administrative arrangements which bore such fruit in England had no parallel'.[14]

Further transatlantic networks of educators and architects were forged during the 1950s. Mary and David Medd spent a full year travelling through the United States and Canada in 1958–9, visiting a large number of schools and colleges. Through their passionate interest in design for education, they established and built important relationships with similarly minded designers, notably W. W. Caudill, John Lyon Reid and Lawrence B. Perkins, who in 1940–41 had led in the design of Crow Island School in Winnetka. This school reinforced the Medds' belief in the importance of designing schools from the inside out, that is, starting from the observable educational needs of the children and teachers and designing from that starting point.

Just before she left for the United States, Mary Medd had designed an inspirational school at Finmere in Oxfordshire for 50 primary-aged children from three rural villages, replacing the dilapidated and unhealthy buildings in which they had previously been educated. Finmere was held to be an exemplary model, setting the

Mary and David Medd meeting with a group of architects to discuss a school plan, Monza, Italy, 1975.

Finmere Infant School, Oxfordshire, 1960; architect Mary Crowley (Medd).

whole trend of primary school design for the 1960s. International commentators later cited it as signifying the changing shape and nature of the primary school. Single-storey, open and light, the school was built on a very small budget to serve a small rural population. The exterior presented a simple form, while the interior was complex and carefully designed to fit the most progressive education in contemporary practice. The school featured two classrooms that could be divided by a moveable screen into different study areas. The plan supported the practice of children working in groups or individually on different sorts of tasks in designated areas. The teachers would support rather than instruct: they would no longer occupy the traditional place allotted to them at the front of the class, but would be freer to move around the classroom in response to perceived needs. The plan allowed for a series of small working areas that offered a degree of seclusion,

Finmere Infant School, site plan.

yet were part of the whole, with access to a larger space in which they could move about freely. There was also the possibility of dividing the space into two or three separate rooms. Finmere was a classic open-plan design, not simply an open space but a carefully designated set of spaces with specific intentions for use and the highest degree of flexibility.[15] This simple and economical design attempted to meet the requirements of teachers according to the new view of the learner as a creative, active and involved participant in the process.

In her earlier fieldwork studies of primary school practice, Mary Medd had noticed that it was becoming increasingly important for groups of children to be able to carry out different projects at different educational levels simultaneously. Edith Moorhouse, senior primary school adviser for Oxfordshire at the time, noted changes in the ways that teachers were reflecting on their practice:

> In the early 1960s . . . it seemed artificial to have physical barriers between infants and juniors as though a line could be drawn between the developments of the six-year-old children in the infant class and the seven-year-olds in the junior class . . . There were also infant teachers who regretted losing contact with the children they knew so well their strengths and weaknesses, at a particularly vulnerable time in their development and who welcomed the opportunity of continuing to work with them in some aspects of learning.[16]

The outcome at Finmere demonstrated for the first time a challenge to the traditional arrangements of the primary school classroom. This was achieved through exhaustive attention to the observed needs of children and teachers and their expression in subtle, modulated spaces, neither completely open nor closed and offering a range of possible arrangements. Crucial features included 'home bays' and spaces such as 'sitting room' and 'kitchen', reflecting a domestic realism in the educational environment. Furnishings emphasized the interior domesticity. The home bay had soft chairs for the children and a rocking chair for the teacher. There was a bedroom that was used for a variety of purposes, some playful and some functional. Its curtain, which could provide privacy, was sometimes used to transform the bedroom into a theatre. Otherwise the space was divided up by means of two folding partitions and a series of fixed wall partitions, creating work bays for a variety of possible uses. Cooperative teaching methods eventually developed in keeping with the design, signified by the tendency for partitions to be left open for much of the time. Moorhouse noted that the background colours were soft and natural – greys, browns, greens and golds, 'a foil for the brightness which the children and their work would introduce'.[17] In November 1965 the Ministry of Housing reconstructed a series of rooms from Finmere for the *International Building Exhibition* at Olympia in London, where it was remarked that 'an almost perfect environment is achieved through careful relation of the building to the needs of children'.[18]

The school design at Finmere was the outcome of a close collaboration between the architect, Mary Medd, and Oxfordshire County Education Authority. Eric Pearson, in his position as national inspector responsible for school building design and development, noted that such collaboration created a high level of confidence in the new open-plan approach to learning in new schools, as well as an enthusiasm for team teaching and cross-disciplinary approaches to the curriculum. This was due to the fact that in Oxfordshire a systematic approach to the training of in-service teachers had been put in place.[19] At Eynsham, where a new school was to be built for 320 pupils in the 5 to 9 age range, teachers specifically asked for the classroom to be 'designed out' of the new school. Theme-based work and groupings in family units required different organizational features from traditional schools. Here, new school buildings were 'gay, light, informal and ultimately domestic, and fashioned carefully to the life and work of the children within'.[20]

Before plans were drawn up for the new school at Eynsham, Edith Moorhouse addressed a group of architects to brief them on what was required. She outlined a series of activities and services to be supported by the building, rather than a list of classrooms allocated for separate ages or specialist subjects. George Baines, the head teacher who led Eynsham primary school through its first decade, remarked that it was essential

> to create a building allowing for as wide a range as possible of children's activities, based upon their needs and interests, to be available at one and the same time, and to do this whilst also creating a building

A lesson at Eynsham Primary School, 1960s.

that gave the possibility of the teachers having recourse to as many known teaching techniques and resources as possible.[21]

David and Mary Medd had visited and sketched the layout of furniture at Brize Norton primary school, a Victorian building opened in 1875, where Baines in his previous headship had carefully reorganized the interior according to his progressive ideas of how children learn. The Medds meticulously followed and noted the activities of the children and the intentions of the teachers throughout a school day. The final design for Eynsham made it difficult to use traditional classroom pedagogy and achieved a synthesis of progressive education and design. There were, for instance, no doors to the home bays. The interior spaces implied and encouraged cooperation in teaching and learning, since their layout suggested that a variety of different sorts of activities might happen at the same time. The materials of the building were configured as teaching tools. For example, the bricks in the hall were exactly 12 inches long and the windows were precisely a yard wide, so that the children could use them for measuring. The internal furnishings and decor were intended to create a child-like environment and to educate. This included special attention to floor surfaces, all designed towards the building being a 'teacher': carpets in home bays and libraries; quarry tiles in the kitchen area and art and craft areas; plastic tiles in the science and practical maths bays; wood blocks in the open areas. Pencil holders and sand trays were made of wood. Soft furnishings included William Morris designs, and some textiles were block-printed by the children. Tables were shaped or coloured to signify their use in the curriculum: black-topped for mathematics, white for practical work, hexagonal for science and round for writing. Such was the level of attention paid to detail that in 1970, when Oxfordshire

Local Educational Authority was unable to supply the correct shape of table at the correct height for children, the deputy head teacher's father was called upon to make wooden extensions to the legs.[22]

This was a school with a strong architectural message and an equally strong philosophical and pedagogical ethos. Baines was an inspirational teacher and a progressive educator. Like many of his predecessors that shared his viewpoint, Baines believed in learning through doing and the importance of engaging the emotions in motivating learning. He justified a redesign of the school community into vertical or 'family' groupings, since this mirrored the hierarchy of the home or of society outside the school. In addition, to his mind, vertical grouping 'overcomes the weakness of age-grouped classes and the evils of ability streaming'. Initially, Eynsham was split into eight vertical groupings, each of the two wings housing four groups and each pupil having one home-bay teacher continuously for four years. Baines placed great emphasis on practical work and on cooperative teaching, and required his staff to keep reflective diaries of their thoughts, feelings, frustrations

Teaching at Eynsham in the 1960s.

and insights. These diaries were like written conversations, and reveal much of the ambience of the place:

> Beginning of Summer term 1970. Tuesday 14th April. Lovely peaceful day. All children seemed happy to be back and settled to work well. Some went immediately to unfinished work. Motivations. A desire to finish work and to see quick results.

> Monday 11th May. Worked in laboratory in morning. Several children working very well with number tracks. Good to see children helping themselves with apparatus. Two of mine off on a study of insects. Mark Evans' idea. Cannot tell what sparked him off. He suddenly decided that was to be his next study.[23]

Eveline Lowe Primary School in Southwark, London, was designed by David and Mary Medd for young children up to the age of 9. When it opened in 1967 it was described as the first truly Plowden Report school and is representative of the kind of detail that interested architects at the time.[24] The buildings were carefully scaled down and loosely grouped to resemble a collection of residences that might be found in a village, reflecting the informality and child-scaled features of Scharoun's school at Lünen and Crowe Island, Winnetka. As David Medd explained, 'the design breaks down what might have been an institutional block into something like a small village that he (the child) can wander around without being aware of the whole'.[25] It was designed with a complete range of furniture, including rocking chairs made by David Medd's father. Medd stipulated in his designs the exact colours, textures and shapes that would give character and comfort to the interior and provide a stimulating learning environment.[26] The interior and exterior spaces for play, study and learning questioned traditional classroom layouts. The school included a 'kiva room' (*kiva* derives from Hopi Indian, meaning retreat or sacred circle), which was rather like a den, simply furnished, with soft carpeted floors and walls lined with wooden bunks, from which the children could choose to listen and look. This space clearly met the needs of the child for social engagement or for a place to withdraw. Throughout the school, institutional arrangements were challenged and domesticity and self-directed learning encouraged.

Innovation in the development of materials and building methods coincided with an era of experimentation with traditional arrangements of time and space. Teachers, particularly in primary schools, explored new approaches to teaching the curriculum and began to experiment with new ways of linking subject learning through topic work.

'Kiva' Eveline Lowe School, London, 1967; architects David and Mary Medd.

Architects spent time in such schools, carefully observing and noting these new approaches, which included, for example, vertical groupings of children (i.e., mixed ages) that required special spatial treatment. They believed – wrongly as it turned out – that they were witnessing the first wave of a genuine and deep-rooted transformation of pedagogy that would embrace all British primary schools and inspire similar schools everywhere in the future.

In designing schools for older children, Henry Morris's notion of the community or village school, established during the 1920s and '30s in Cambridgeshire in England, with its arms embracing the community and its features of open access, was reinterpreted during the 1960s and '70s by a new generation of architects eager to combine the arts of town planning and educational design. In Nottinghamshire, Henry Swain, who had worked in Hertfordshire just after the war until 1955, set about inspiring a team of architects and engineers to design and build community schools. Rather like the Hertfordshire teams of architects and educational planners, the Local Educational Authority was able to provide a platform that would encourage innovation to benefit not only the locality but also other parts of the country.

Outdoor spaces for play, Eveline Lowe School.

Swain and his colleagues, committed to the community school concept, set out to consider the needs of children and teachers, and then to find new ways of applying the benefits of mass-produced construction to individual school buildings. At Sutton-in-Ashfield, for example, the more usual concept of a comprehensive school set amid isolating playing fields was replaced by one positioned in the middle of the town, directly connected with a community centre and other public facilities. Like almost everything under Swain's aegis, it was built using radical new engineering technologies designed by the team, which enabled the school buildings to be erected quickly and cheaply using prefabricated materials. The Consortium of Local Authorities' Special Programme (CLASP) resulted in hundreds of schools being built according to this system of design during the late 1950s and '60s in England, and,

'Domestic' interior space at Eveline Lowe School.

though not considered great architecture, CLASP was among the most radical architectural projects of the decade, achieved through the desire of architects at this time to work for the public sector. During these years, it was the public sector, at least in England, that provided the platform for innovation and development.

Architects practising during these years were often motivated by the mood of the time that celebrated and embraced both the arts and technology as liberating forces for change and for good. They were also motivated to develop new materials and techniques to enable schools to be built quickly, economically and efficiently, as the pressure on school places mounted as a result of the post-war baby boom. Nottinghamshire was subject to subsidence caused by past mine workings, which posed a technological and engineering challenge. The answer was a light steel frame, with spring-braces to deal with soil movements. Henry Swain was appointed County

Interior of a small CLASP primary school built for and exhibited at the 1960 Triennale at Milan; architect Henry Swain.

Architect in 1964, and developed the system alongside a mechanical engineer, Lister Heathcote. The system was extended to other counties with subsidence problems. As Andrew Saint put it, Swain 'for nearly 30 years, incarnated the conscience of the CLASP'.[27]

A small CLASP school, built for the Milan Triennale of 1960, set British school architecture on the international agenda when it won first prize. The school was built in eight weeks on site and afterwards was donated to the Milan Civic Authorities. It was furnished meticulously for the exhibition. Children's work, materials and activities were represented, indicating that a school building was never complete without the human elements of interaction made evident. These British developments did have some followers. A few CLASP schools were built on the Continent, notably in Portugal, while in the United States thirteen schools were built under the School Construction Systems Development (SCSD) programme in California, which was started in Palo Alto in 1961 by the architect Ezra Ehrenkrantz. The SCSD required all services to be carried clear of the floors, to maintain flexibility in planning. The open-plan schools developed in the USA from the 1970s were largely indebted to the SCSD.[28]

The Newsom Report *Half Our Future*, published in 1963, betrayed an anxiety about the ways in which many children and young people were left behind by an educational system that did not recognize or understand their needs. The physical spaces of the school, their design and scale in the context of particular urban environments, were thought to be crucial in bringing about change in order to combat disaffection and anti-social behaviour. Many of the ideas about the flexible use of school buildings, first voiced in the interwar years, were revisited during this period. There were economic arguments, such as those voiced by the Ministry of Education, which suggested:

Society is no longer prepared to make available a set of valuable buildings and resources for the exclusive use of a small, arbitrarily defined sector of the community, to be used seven hours a day for two-thirds of the year. School buildings have to be regarded therefore as a resource for the total community available to many different groups, used for many different purposes and open if necessary twenty four hours a day.[29]

It was hoped that the school at the heart of the community would keep alive and develop in many ways the ideas and experiments originated by John Dewey in Chicago, Henry Morris in Cambridgeshire and Edward O'Neill in Lancashire. Like the Hertfordshire schools, local state planning in England at this time demonstrated a unique close cooperation between architects and educators. The notion that the school plant might become the most important cultural and educational hub of a community, whose borders and boundaries were open to the world and whose facilities were used by all sorts of people of all ages at all times, emerged strongly at this time of commitment to architecture as a public service; this was a vision of school as a place of friendship and happiness, community and cooperation, rather than fear and dread.

In 1965 the British Government formally endorsed comprehensive education as national policy, and new comprehensive schools emerged in towns and cities across England.[30] Particularly radical designs were produced for buildings in progressive Local Education Authorities. In Leicestershire, Countesthorpe Community College, for children aged 14 to 16, was opened in 1970. How far the circular design by architects Farmer and Dark signalled a break with the past and an emphasis on distributed leadership and power in learning environments is difficult to judge. Stewart Mason, director of education in Leicestershire, was well aware of the pioneering work of the development teams, which had signalled changes in the arrangement of space and time for learning in schools for younger children. He wanted to harness a similarly transforming climate to the design of schools for older children. He suggested that it was vital for leading administrators to 'study what is actually happening, to define the directions in which ideas and practices appear to be moving and to try to project these trends a few years ahead'.[31] Tim McMullen, the first principal of Countesthorpe, wrote in 1969:

> We have a chance to rethink the total process of learning within a school . . . This does not mean that everything we do will be different from what has been done before, but it should mean that we do not automatically repeat an established practice without considering why.[32]

McMullen and Mason were intent on drawing on the best of practice in the pioneering schools for younger children and thereby transforming education for the older child. This meant challenging the divisions between subject knowledge, promoting team teaching and breaking down hierarchies and age-related structures, all of which were reflected in the arrangements of classrooms and departments.

Countesthorpe, which became well known for its innovative approach to the curriculum, the development of smaller communities within the larger school and the attempt to include children in running the affairs of the school, is less known for its attractive and unusual building design. The circular building contained a predominantly open-plan arrangement of space with some pod-like spaces off the central area. Over time, these were removed and replaced by classrooms as the commitment to the open-learning ethos weakened. But originally, as Brian Simon, at that time a

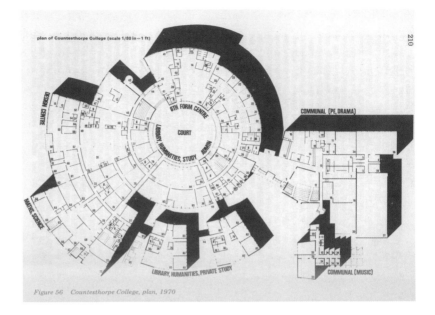

plan of Countesthorpe College (scale 1/80 in — 1 ft)

DESIGN CENTRE

MATHS SCIENCE

6TH FORM CENTRE

COURT

LIBRARY, HUMANITIES, STUDY

ADMIN

LIBRARY, HUMANITIES, PRIVATE STUDY

COMMUNAL (PE, DRAMA)

COMMUNAL (MUSIC)

Figure 56   Countesthorpe College, plan, 1970

leading educational academic and a governor of the college, recalled that

> the building was designed to include facilities for youth and adult community activities on a single site; but there were other considerations affecting the final design of the building which originated in the experience of comprehensive education. Instead of the usual rows of box like classrooms, Leicestershire had already begun to erect secondary school buildings on an open plan basis, allowing for team (co-operative) teaching and individual and group activities of various sizes as well as class or larger groupings. This concept was based on the resources approach to learning, which represented a shift from class teaching as the normal mode to individual and group work and what is sometimes called the discovery approach to learning.[33]

Countesthorpe Community College, Leicestershire, 1970, architects Farmer and Dark.

As chief education officer for Leicestershire, Stewart Mason had set out to achieve the design of a building that would facilitate and suggest interdisciplinary work, and a circular shape was chosen to help amplify the interconnectedness of the various disciplines. Respectful and warm relations between pupils and teachers were emphasized through the design, and Countesthorpe took seriously the idea of pupil voice. Far from being a cold, institutionalized space, it was intended that those entering the building would note this warmth and sense the unity of purpose. The college was visited by many teachers from the UK and abroad during its first years of operation, and the experience of training or working there left a life-long impression on students and staff.

Pimlico Comprehensive, which also opened in 1970, was a purpose-built comprehensive school situated in south-west London. Designed for more than 1,000 pupils, it was conceived by architects Hubert Bennett, Michael Powell and John Bancroft on a 'heroic scale'. In 1973 the Buildings of England volume on London described it as the

> weirdest recent building of London, very long, placed along the middle axis of the site, with play areas to N and S. It is of four storeys, the lowest being below pavement level. Raw concrete and glass, all the glazing sloping as in hothouses. And will there not be a hothouse effect, at least on the S side? The long frontages step forward and backward in a restless, aggressive, exciting way . . . The people have taken over.[34]

As the writer feared, the pupils and teachers froze in winter and sizzled in summer. Nevertheless, the architecture reflected a confidence in the comprehensive ideal and apparently signified a radical change in the approach to learning and teaching in a new era. While the building itself appeared to be progressive, however, the

pedagogy adhered to the traditional, and this was reflected in the interior organization of space. At the time when its brief was being drawn up, in 1965, the new purpose-built comprehensive schools were coming under fire, since commentators were quick to condemn the shift from a selective system of secondary education. As Pimlico was opening, the backlash had already begun with the publication of the Black Papers that severely criticized the contemporary progressive ideals in primary and secondary education in England and Wales.[35] Plans for Pimlico had begun ten years after the opening of the first purpose-built comprehensive school in England, Kidbrooke School for Girls in south-east London, a school that had attracted controversy as a showcase of the comprehensive system in practice. Hence, the conservatism built into

Pimlico Comprehensive School, London, 1970; architects Hubert Bennett, Michael Powell and John Bancroft.

the design of Pimlico could be read against this backdrop of criticism and damnation, which prevented the full experimentation with alignments of space and time that may have radically altered the experience of learning and teaching in the secondary school. After five years of operation, the critic and educationalist Colin Ward commented that as 'architectural sculpture' Pimlico School was 'a *tour de force*', but he feared that its approach to education failed to match the quality of its architecture.[36]

To some, Pimlico appeared to represent the end of an era rather than the start of a new one. Unlike Countesthorpe, the design was based on a typical curriculum of the 1960s, entirely subject-based and accepting the traditional classroom as the typical organizational device. The brief had assumed traditional didactic methods and had made no attempt to encourage thought and action around cooperative learning, cross-disciplinary approaches to the curriculum or individual or self-directed learning. The post-occupancy evaluation, published in 1975, revealed disappointment that the building had not met the basic requirements thought necessary for the well-being of pupils. It was asked: 'how do individual children find security and an identity in this school' where there was 'limited privacy and peace?' The school could clearly not be understood by its architecture alone. It was understood only through an appreciation of how it developed and shaped itself in the course of its daily function. Pimlico School, while a celebrated model of engineering and architecture during the 1970s, seems to demonstrate that buildings do matter, but that in this example the final design did little to capitalize on approaches to teaching and learning that would underpin the comprehensive and progressive ideal.

Schools, however they are designed, are inhabited spaces, and although there were exceptions, most teachers were ill-prepared for working in radically changed environments, and their initial training and preparation for a lifetime of professional service did not seriously consider the matter of the material conditions of the spaces they would occupy. In 1974 a report published by the National Union of Teachers (NUT) (England) noted the most popular complaints, which more often than not included noise nuisance. In research studies that followed in the USA, where half of all schools built between 1967 and 1969 were open-plan, and in Europe, it was concluded that architectural design does not fundamentally determine teacher practice, but that teachers determine and arrange their spaces in accordance with their perceived needs, habits and beliefs – hence the practice of erecting walls and other barriers in originally planned open spaces to bring about a return to a classroom environment. In his study of primary school design published in 1972, Malcolm Seaborne noted that the financial constraints that governments placed on the design of new schools during these years did not enable the experiment to be explored fully. This, together with the reluctance of many teachers to let go of tried and tested approaches to teaching in the classroom, doomed the open-plan school to failure. By the mid-1970s government pressure in Britain was growing against the freedom of experimentation and innovation that had been enjoyed by teachers for more than a decade.[37]

The extent to which experimentation and innovation in school design can break with the traditions of the past is limited by the simple fact that while new models are developed and built for the few, most children will continue to require a place to be educated. In reality, there is never a sufficient break with the past, and to some extent this may explain the re-emergence of tradition in school design. While schools did emerge that had shed their customary corridors and classrooms, and that invited cooperative and collaborative learning, there was never the likelihood that more than a minority of teachers and children would experience such a reorganization of space in their school careers. As a consequence, there always existed a time lag between innovation in school building design and teacher training and professional development, towards new forms of pedagogical practise that considered use of space and time in alternative ways. In spite of the innovations of the 1960s and '70s, apart from a few exceptions, little changed in the preparation of teachers as professionals within open and expanded learning environments.

4 Aligning Architecture and Education – Building Schools 'That Fit'

> Our vast secondary schools are among the last great Fordist institutions, where people in large numbers go at the same time, to work in the same place, to a centrally devised schedule announced by the sound of a bell.[1]

Since the 1990s government policies in neo-liberal economies have instituted a much greater bureaucratization of the teaching profession. One of the consequences has been a reduction in the time available to teachers for experimentation, risk-taking and what some have called utopian thinking.[2] Combined with this, changes in the nature of the relationship between parents and teachers from one of mutual trust towards contractual obligation have helped to give rise to the notion of education as a commodity. The rise in levels of anxiety about risk in school environments and out-of-school educational trips has limited the ways in which teachers have been able to overcome the harshness of the institution through the development of personal and affectionate relationships with pupils, becoming a second parent and meeting their emotional needs. Meanwhile, schools have become transformed through widespread government commitment to computer-supported learning, but not always in ways that benefit all those who occupy school buildings for large parts of their days. Classrooms, not originally designed with computers in mind, have often become cluttered, over-heated spaces. Most commentators argue that in spite of the appearance of change, the school remains remarkably intact as an institution. This has led to a return to the question of scale in designing for learning.

McCauley Junior High School in Edmonton, Alberta, Canada, was constructed almost a century ago and has operated as a school ever since. The original design is monumental, signalling in its symmetrical façade the gender division that was an accepted part of schooling at the time of its construction. Completed in 1911, it was designed by George Pheasey in partnership with a Mr Batson. Pheasey, originally from Derbyshire in the UK, oversaw the construction of six schools in Edmonton during these years. Like many schools built during this era across the world, the building in its original design suggests an education designed for the twentieth century rather than for the twenty-first. Unusually, however, when considering re-design, the authorities in Edmonton decided that rather than tear down and remove the original school the past should be acknowledged as an important link with the present. Within the reception area is a pronounced display of educational

McCauley School, Edmonton, Canada, 1911; architect George Pheasey. Re-design by Neils Gerbitz, 2006.

technology from the past: an original slate mounted on the wall, the original terrazzo flooring and old photographs and artefacts. The main hallway has been made narrower to make way for offices for community agencies, so that they may have a visible presence in the school – a community health nurse and a family therapist. The stairwells have kept the original stairs and banisters (the risers came from the Carnegie steel mill in Pittsburgh in 1911), but the stairway now features ceramic tiles on the walls. Corridors have been widened, giving ample space for movement and storage for pupils' possessions. The washrooms, which originally and until recently were located in the basement, have been modernized and are now on every floor, where the hand-washing / sink space is open to the hallway and only the actual cubicles have doors on them. The interior of this rectangular building, which still contains many original features, is softened through curved walls and surfaces, creating a more human scale in this otherwise large school.

This is a school that through reconstruction remembers its past and celebrates its heritage. The interior has been carefully reshaped by the architect Niels Gerbitz, paying attention to the needs of pupils and their families and with careful attention to detail, challenging the institutional while embracing it fully, and,

Interiors at McCauley School, Edmonton, Alberta, 2006.

by making the original structure clearly observable, transcending it. Rebuilding and restoring such environments, while preserving previous designs that were at one time answers to the question of education, can enhance the engagement of the school community with the school building.

How can the history of educational thinking, practice and school design be brought to bear on the design of schools for the future? Architects and educators with an active interest in designing effective and engaging learning environments are concerned, as ever, with the challenge of aligning architecture and education. But how many architects today are able to follow the advice of pioneering collaborations of educators and architects from the past and actually spend time in schools, carefully observing how they function in order to understand how best to support good

Bishops Park College, Clacton, Essex, 2005; architects Lloyd Stratton of ACP Architects CoPartnership.

practice? Frameworks for collaboration, sponsored by national governments and facilitated through local authorities, and therefore able to carry out research and development, are no longer in place. It is no longer standard practice to carry out the type of post-occupancy evaluations done by the Medds in the UK during the 1950s and '60s and published as building bulletins. It is more usual today for architects to gain government contracts through competitive tendering and through offering the most economical brief.

While McCauley Junior School retains elements of its architectural past, Bishops Park College, a new-build co-educational community comprehensive school in Clacton-on-Sea, Essex, has designed arrangements of time and space to support the curriculum in a manner reminiscent of the experimental pedagogy of the 1970s. Opened in 2002, in temporary accommodation, Bishops Park is attempting to redefine what we might mean by a 'school' for the twenty-first century and at the same time is intent to remember and embrace innovations and experimentations carried out in comprehensive schools during the 1970s. The opportunity to collaborate in the design process enabled the head teacher to explore the history of innovation in student-centred pedagogy and apply them in new conditions. The college is divided into three mini-schools where staff teams, responsible collectively for the whole curriculum, teach most of the lessons to a smaller community of learners. The curriculum is managed in a way that celebrates specialization through regular master classes, but sees teachers as generalists first, experts in pedagogy. The timetable is complex and unusual: on one day every week, children are taught one subject only. A new building was designed for the college to provide a major community focus, including a community library, nursery and a centre for the over-sixties. As such, this is the first purpose-designed 'school within a school' layout in the UK since the 1970s. While in the past such a design was associated with progressive education, today it is thought to assist in tailoring education to individual pupils' needs and to meet the personalization agenda. That said, the challenge to traditional forms of school organization and an interdisciplinary approach to knowledge are in the progressive tradition. The school is designed around the pupils, the teachers and the community – not educational subjects.[3]

This is a school that is well aware of the historical legacy of experimentation with time and space in the creation of radically altered learning environments. The design brief for the new building specifically called for a human-scale environment in line with the argument that

> if schools are to continue to exist well into the twenty-first century they need to be more fulfilling, more creative and more humanly attentive places than they have been thus far, both for those who teach in them and for those required to attend them.[4]

The design received the RIBA East Architecture for Education Award in 2005. The architects wrote:

> The design and character created has taken inspiration from the coastal character of the local area, helping to provide a strong connection between the aesthetic of the new school and its local context. This has influenced the design, from the colours of the building elevations (based on those found on the brightly coloured beach huts) to the materials, features and planting styles adopted. Thus a 'fresh air and sea breeze' quality is intended to symbolize an optimistic and bright future for the new school which includes some substantially deprived areas within its catchment.
>
> The school is designed to create an exciting, stimulating and

unusual environment. It was important to have lots of natural policing and good site lines with open staircases, large atria, large windows that together produce a light and airy feel to the school with good visual interconnectivity.[5]

Bishops Park College in England and McCauley School in Canada are examples of two different design approaches that acknowledge the past in order to transcend it. Schools operating today are rich territories of past educational activity and experience. In that sense, 'buildings remember the story of their making'.[6]

Schools functioning at the turn of the millennium in most senses resemble schools constructed around the turn of the last century. On the whole, children still move en masse at regular intervals, interrupted by the bell, and are disgorged into corridors all at the same time. They are still separated and segregated according to notions of ability, and 'we still largely define success as the consequence of sitting at a small table and writing furiously for two or three hours'.[7] At the same time, the locus of learning is shifting and some commentators have argued that the frontline of learning is no longer the classroom but the home – particularly the bedroom and living room. The introduction of information and communication technologies has given the impression of modernization and change, but, apart from some notable exceptions, the essential elements of school remain – buildings, classrooms, corridors, timetables, bells and security devices. At the Microsoft School of the Future in Philadelphia, pupils and their bags are screened on arrival as if boarding a flight at an international airport. Such high-tech responses to scrutiny and surveillance betray a heightened state of anxiety about the capacity of young people to unleash destruction within schools. Surveillance cameras are ubiquitous in the United States, after a series of violent attacks perpetrated by children on their fellow students and teachers during the 1990s and 2000s.

While wanting a safe and secure place to learn, however, children and young people have voiced their concerns that school can sometimes feel 'too secure'. A poll carried out by the UK-based organization School Works in 2006 revealed that while most children did feel that their schools were safe, sometimes they felt that this created a prison-like climate:

> My school is perhaps a bit too secure looking. It seems like it is a prison. There are tall red fences everywhere and it's not very attractive. We feel like caged animals. Perhaps they could think of a nicer looking but practical way to make it secure without being ugly.[8]

The respondents used the prison analogy a number of times in their answers. When considering the point of view of children as the principal users of school buildings, we might ask: 'Do security fences make children feel safe or imprisoned? Does CCTV create a sense of protection or a feeling of being watched?'[9]

Government policies responsible for the production of 'schools for the future' talk of transforming learning environments to

The School of the Future, Philadelphia, sponsored by Microsoft; architects The Prisco Group. Opened 2006.

Inside the School of the Future.

become fit for the twenty-first century, but somehow struggle to do so. New school types such as 'Specialist Schools', 'Academies' and 'Charter schools', which are beginning to replace public schools in parts of Europe and the USA, suggest radical change and often incorporate new build. In practice, however, schools already designed and completed in the twenty-first century demonstrate continuity in design rather than radical change. Apart from some significant exceptions discussed here, there appears to be a reluctance to revisit the open-learning ethos of the past, in spite of sound arguments that favour collaborative and interdisciplinary approaches in the context of 'lifelong learning'. Review of subject- and specialist-based curricula and recognition of the possibilities and value of interdisciplinary studies suggest, once again, the need for an alternative relationship between time and space in schools and a freeing up of the rigidity of the curriculum. In the main, however, there is a strong persistence in the design of regularly shaped classrooms grouped around larger halls and connecting corridors. This will continue as long as the overriding focus is on pupil achievement through standardized testing.

Habits and practices, approaches and beliefs acquired through dominant cultures of schooling remain strong in the shaping of school environments. Schools are usually strictly hierarchical institutions, where power relations are regarded as crucial to the proper functioning of the learning and teaching community. The organization of spaces within the school, such as the layout of learning areas, can emphasize these power relations or offer a challenge to them. On the whole, decision-making about the use of space, the arrangement of time and the incorporation of material objects for teaching and learning continues to reside with the classroom teacher and the school head. Apart from some exceptions explored in this chapter, children's participation in spatial

design is minimal or tokenistic. At the same time, the training of teachers rarely includes a perspective that encourages and enhances an interest in the ecological aspects of pedagogy and the management of space for different modalities of teaching and learning.

There is now recognition that children and young people play an active role in shaping their social identities and environments, and as such are competent members of society whose voices should be heard. Such a shift in the view of the child, and of childhood itself, has produced some good evidence and overwhelming support for extending the means by which they can participate in the institutions associated with their lives, particularly schools. This is an important and significant shift in ideals and aspirations. Very few children attending school today, however, anywhere in the world, are aware that they have the right, under the United Nations Convention on the Rights of the Child (UNCRC) of 1989, to express their opinions, ideas and views concerning their lives in general and their education in particular. The decades since the

Children view a school plan, from C. G. Stillman and R. Castle Cleary, *The Modern School* (1949).

ratification of the UNCRC have witnessed a reassertion of the notion of children's participation in decision making and a range of practical efforts to achieve it, with, it has to be said, a somewhat chequered result. While the views, tastes and inclinations of the young are regularly and frequently surveyed and sampled, there is evidence that children and young people have yet to be convinced that their right to have a say is now, or ever has been, genuinely respected. For many children, school remains an experience to be endured over the long haul. The designed environment, and the way that teachers interpret it as a space for delivering the curriculum and administering tests and assessments, reminds them of their place in the established educational hierarchy.

Some of the most innovative and pioneering efforts to include children in the design of school environments have been carried out with very young ones. In the UK, Peter Moss and Alison Clark have developed theories and practical methodologies that enable children to unleash their talents for building and design in collaboration with architects, either planning new nurseries or redesigning existing ones.[10] The Mosaic approach involves children showing their view of the spaces through walking tours, photography, mapping, observation and discussion. In Italy, Michele Zini, an architect and researcher with Reggio Children and Domus Academy Research Centre, has pioneered new directions in enabling adults and children to collaborate in decision making about their learning environments. When the 3-year-olds at the Giacosa Infant school in Milan arrive on their first day, they are greeted with an open, empty space. They then work with adults to 'dress' the rooms, deciding together what furnishings to place and how to arrange a structured and decorated space. Zini suggests that the school or early learning centre

is an ever changing environment where design, furnishing, systems and interfaces must allow different activities in the same place at different times of the day, without a pre-determined programme but based on the decisions made by children and teachers at a particular time.[11]

Colours used in the interior should, Zini adds, go beyond the simple red, yellow and blue that adults traditionally associate with children. 'Subtle shades, contrasts and variety add visual richness.' Such ideas are in keeping with a new view of childhood that reflects critically on past certainties and expectations, and attempts to afford respect to childlike perspectives.

It is rare that one's time at school as a pupil coincides with a period of massive state investment in the educational infrastructure. The beginning of the twenty-first century is just such a time in many parts of Europe, North America and across the world, as nations grapple with the implications, for the designed learning environment, of the technological revolution in information and

State nursery and infant school, San Felice, Modena, Italy; architects ZPZ Partners.

communications. Many factors are at play in envisaging the new learning environments of the twenty-first century. Economic drivers have introduced new partnerships between the public and private sectors that reduce the capital investment of the state and promote a free market in the development of new schools and the rebuilding of old ones. This buoyant new market is stimulating competition. It has also led to the renewal of the notion, held at the crest of each wave of previous periods of investment, that buildings can and will transform education. Meanwhile, new theories of childhood, and challenges to established notions of child development through age and stage, e.g., Piagetian theory, play to a new design interest that celebrates the capacity of the young as knowledge producers; it seeks an architecture that questions the formal boundaries between child and adult and that reminds us of the rights of the child to have access to culture, creativity and means of free expression. There has also been renewed interest in physiology and neurology in relation to the learning process, which is reflected in an interest in designing learning environments that mirror and amplify the emotions, the ways that memory works, individual learning styles and the mechanism of brain function.[12]

All of this suggests to some a need for the freeing up of space and a removal of predetermined adult-centric pedagogical cues, such as the classroom *per se*. The architect and educational designer Bruce A. Jilk in the USA has argued that there has been a tendency in the past to over-design schools, and that designers need to reconsider their preoccupation with suggesting all the functions for the teaching and learning environment. Jilk suggests a 'montage of gaps' to draw attention to the significance of the spaces and places in between the formal learning environments; these can be left incomplete in order to stimulate a continuous

design response among the users of these spaces over time. (His school at Ingunnarskóli in Reykjavík, Iceland, which was completed in 2005, is discussed below.) The environmental psychologist Roger Hart, who has drawn attention to the natural capacities of children as designers and builders, argues that 'we need to redesign the forgotten spaces where informal learning occurs: school yards and lunchrooms'.[13] This suggests that a reconfiguration of the school is necessary if we are to acknowledge that these are indeed children's spaces and to recognize the fact that children also learn when they are not at school.

Contemporary interpretations of child-centred education are therefore imbued with an emerging new understanding of childhood itself. The interpretation or definition of child-centredness is dependent on changing ideas about what the child is, and how the place of learning should be configured. At the turn of the millennium, the notion that children are powerful agents in constructing their social worlds is influencing the interpretation of child-centred education. Participation in the design and build of the learning

Hampden Gurney Primary School, Westminster, London, 2002; architects Building Design Partnership.

environment is becoming a particularly important factor in making schools attractive to the current generation of young people. The child as innovator, researcher and designer, in partnership with professional practitioners, is regarded as a legitimate presence in shaping and influencing the school of the future.

Some architects today work closely with children in participatory design relationships. One such architect is Peter Hübner, who sees the school as a 'self-designed habitat for teachers and taught' and 'an interaction process between teachers, pupils and ideally parents as well, as a piece of life activity for all concerned'.[14] Hübner is professor at the architecture faculty of Stuttgart University, and has been running an architecture practice in the nearby town of Neckartenzlingen for 30 years. Since the last decades of the twentieth century he has demonstrated how children and young people can participate as designers and experts in renewal, recycling and restoration. In the process of drawing up the final scheme, he uses children's designs in drawings and in modelling. In *Kinder Bauen Ihre Schule* (*Children Make Their School*),

One view of pupil participation in school design.

Hübner has argued that a new concept of 'school' (one which changes in time, demonstrates concepts of sustainability and has a differentiated form accepting the creative contribution of staff and children) is needed for twenty-first-century requirements.

Hübner's Morgenstern Schule at Reutlingen (1987) was constructed out of recycled materials, namely the framework of sheds which had been part of a Porsche factory removed and reconstructed. In collaboration with the school community, these ugly structures were reshaped to fit the principles and philosophy of anthroposophy practised in the Waldorf (Steiner) School. The result was a beautiful polygonal building with a central theatre. However ecological it may have been, economically the use of recycled materials failed to compensate for the high labour costs.

Schools that 'fit' the environment, that serve as examples of sustainable living and that educate the community about its relationship with the natural world are desirable and beautiful spaces. They appear to 'fit' the child's view of the desirable school of the future: 'A beautiful school: A comfortable school: A safe school: A

Morgenstern School, Reutlingen, Germany, 1986; architect Peter Hübner.

'School as a Planet', drawn by a 14-year-old, from Catherine Burke and Ian Grosvenor, *The School I'd Like* (2003).

listening school: A flexible school: A relevant school: A respectful school: A school without walls: A school for everybody'. These were the wishes of the children and young people in the UK who participated in the *School I'd Like* competition in 2001, expressing their opinions and describing their vision of a school for the future.[15] These are the challenges posed to architects, educational-ists and learners, who together might realize this vision through pedagogical and material re-design.

The environmental educator David Orr has said: 'our education up till now has in some ways created a monster'.[16] He suggests that a crucial and urgent question in the debate about educational futures is that of survival and planetary sustainability. He argues that the epistemological framework used up to now, based on the separation of forms of knowledge, can lead only to ecological dis-aster. The voices from *School I'd Like* in 2001 appear to recognize this. These schoolchildren seem unconvinced that an academic curriculum relying on the traditional separation of the arts from the sciences and the latest technologies will equip them for life in the twenty-first century. They view themselves as global citizens, whose futures may lie in any part of the world. Metaphors of planetary exploration betray a curiosity and consciousness about the enormity and complexity of human experience and knowledge. They are aware of the diversity of peoples, their cultures and the richness and depth of their histories, to a far greater extent than previous generations, and the ideas they present reflect an eagerness to dig deep, to meet challenges, to explore and survive. The exterior design of Peter Hübner's JUFO Youth Centre at Moglingen, near Stuttgart in Germany, resembles a space ship that has just landed, and suggests the possibilities of space travel through advances in technologies. As such, the concept is driven by a young person's vision of an exciting and stimulating environment. Inside, however, an equally appropriate and highly sensory childlike environment is found, shaped by young hands and built largely of mud. 'Within the clear unified envelope is an irregular city of mud, hand-built and decorated as a live project'.[17]

The need for flexible solutions in school design is almost a mantra in the history of education. Despite their poor record of success, designers of learning environments somehow continue to argue the same case. Ultimately, schools are complex organisms of human relationships, and their interconnectivity is opposed to individual innovation. An expanded range of pedagogical possibilities

Space craft: a youth club in Moglingen, Germany; architect Peter Hübner.

is required of the school building for the twenty-first century. While in the past configurations of teachers and learners in spaces included teacher instruction, individual group work and project-based learning, the impact of new technologies, combined with new theories of learning and intelligences, have extended the list of possibilities to include technology-based learning with mobile computers, distance learning and research via the Internet with wireless networking. Emerging ideas that are influencing both policy and practice include 'engagement' (making the curriculum meaningful and motivating), 'personalization' (tailoring the curriculum to each learner), 'connectivity' (using and encouraging good social relationships), 'authenticity' (making learning real), 'technological enhancement' (using technology in learning), 'lifelong learning' (focusing on learning at all ages), 'facilitation' (guiding or scaffolding learning), 'accountability' (meeting high standards), 'equity' (ensuring equal opportunity to learn), 'accessibility' (access to learning at any time), creativity (encouraging knowledge production) and investment (learning as the key to economic prosperity). Some consider that it is vital to harness the emotions in learning and to understand the complexities of brain function. The notion that schools provide comprehensive knowledge and that only schools provide opportunities for learning is becoming replaced by an acknowledgement that learning can and does happen at any time and in any place. Moreover, it is now being recognized that learning is most successful when learner and teacher share control of the learning pace and place. The city, village or town as a metaphor for school has re-emerged strongly in contemporary design discourse. The city is at once an inclusive environment, serving the community in all its physical, emotional and spiritual needs, and a dynamic and ever changing phenomenon. It is the emblem of all that is modern, the gateway to culture and a place full of energy and opportunity. Ideally, it is a democratic space that is managed by some on behalf of the whole community, so enabling the individual to navigate freely and independently. This book has noted such metaphors at earlier dates, for example during the 1950s and '60s, when schools were designed using the small town and streets metaphor as a signifier of progressivism. Once more, the traditional double-ranked (i.e. with classrooms on each side) corridor, with classrooms leading off, has been replaced in school design by the idea of the 'learning street'.

The learning street is considered to function not only as a means of getting from one place to another, but also as an enhancer of social connectivity. Unlike the corridor, the 'learning street' resembles a city street, containing a variety of spaces and places from which to choose activities and materials as needed; areas where the material products of learning are displayed and marketed; spaces where learners may practise their skills in providing a service to the community; and regions where various nooks and crannies are conducive to and supportive of social interaction. The 'learning street' is differently designed from the corridor. It should be sufficiently wide to suggest multi-function and there should be ample natural daylight available, as in a real thoroughfare. At its best, the school 'learning street' really does suggest the school as a self-sufficient dynamic community. Peter Hübner conceives of the school as a highly differentiated little town: 'A street instead of a corridor, houses not classrooms, a town hall, not offices. A village, in fact, with a theatre and an inn'. Learning streets, however, can occur almost as afterthoughts or gestures towards the school as a city. The Capital City Academy, in Brent, London, was designed by Norman Foster Partners and opened in September 2003. The aim was to create a building to inspire young people to learn, given its location in an area of much defection from schooling:

> A central spine organises the building, forming a spacious internal street that runs through the centre of the school to allow visual connections and interaction in a stable and safe environment. The concern for transparency and openness was paramount, with classrooms that are larger and taller than usual with partially glazed walls, which provide natural lighting and visual links between classrooms and departments, and natural cross-ventilation to the exterior.
>
> The Academy has been designed to provide flexible learning opportunities and can be reconfigured as teaching and learning practices evolve in the future. Restaurant facilities are located at the heart of the building to encourage social interaction. A generous full-length colonnade embraces the sports field and relates the building to the surrounding landscape.[18]

To the eye of an architect, the entrance has a classical stamp, updated with a Corbusier-style pilotis. To the eye of a child, the entrance perhaps resembles a supermarket or an airport; and indeed so much attention is paid to on-site security that the electronic gates and swipe-card turnstiles do suggest something other than a school in the traditional sense. Among the main design features are the passages described as 'street[s]', which stretch through the length of the building as a central spine. Transparency and openness means that much natural light penetrates the interior, but there are few small intimate socializing spaces and there is a sense that there is nowhere to hide. The 'street' billows and flows like a blue ribbon, suggesting the flow of information and knowledge. In fact, however, apart from providing a little more width, it is not very far removed in function from the traditional

corridor, which suggests that behaviour in it will be little altered. There is a clear danger that the schools designed in the twenty-first century for the future are turning out to be 'new old schools'.[19]

Interior 'street' with classrooms off, Capital City Academy, London; architects Norman Foster Group.

In schools such as these we see once again the concern to contain, discipline and protect the schoolchild. There are few places to hide in such an environment, and the all-seeing eye of the teacher is enhanced through basic materials – glass walls and partitions – and technology. Tragedies across the developed world involving breaches of school security, resulting in large-scale injury and loss of life, such as the Columbine school shooting, have increased anxieties about the safety of children on school premises, and designers have to achieve a difficult balance between an architecture that both embraces the community and reassures it that its children will be safe at school. Schools have never been immune from violence and aggression, but today there is a greater degree of sophistication in the security devices designed to reduce risk. The twenty-first-century school increasingly has to tout for custom, and such technology can help to sell the school to prospective parents who are offered 'choice' between state schools.

The persistence of the classroom as a space for learning is perhaps one indication of how issues of surveillance, discipline and control continue to dominate school environments. Where there is no commitment to, or belief in, an open and flexible curriculum and associated pedagogy, as is demonstrated in Bishops Park College in England, the tendency is to return to the classroom as a familiar territory. Schools envisaged as open plan and opened during the first decade of the twenty-first century have in practice reverted to classroom organization through the erection of walls. In the USA, however, as was the case in England during the 1950s and '60s, there are districts that have wholeheartedly committed resources to a belief in open and flexible learning environments. The state of Minnesota has led the way in designing schools that question the traditional divisions between teachers and learners and classroom-based pedagogy. This has permitted a significant shift in the public (i.e., state) school ethos of the area and has stimulated some interesting experimentation. Stone Bridge Elementary School, Stillwater, Minnesota, for example, takes for its slogan 'We build bridges instead of walls'.[20]

In the main, the Minnesota schools have a commitment to an interdisciplinary curriculum, and so they are wedded to a principle of structured, open and self-directed learning. They are designed to support a unique curriculum which utilizes partnerships with outside agencies such as the state zoo. Many have customized furniture for flexibility – desks on casters with lockable spaces – emphasizing respect for the students' work. Vertical pin-board surfaces, attached to these desks, allow for privacy when seated; whiteboards on the other sides of the pin-boards enable work stations to be moved in order to configure group-learning spaces when required. As in Bishops Park College, the idea of a school within a school is found here. The organization of the students into 'houses' breaks down the student group into social settings, and further subdivision into 'pods' is indicated in the built environment, enabling teams of teachers to work with the same groups of students in the long term. Time is organized in large chunks. There may be three hours for interdisciplinary instruction at the core, while subject-based instruction, as discrete class instruction, is realized at the periphery and arranged as needed. These schools do not have the bells or sirens, still found in most schools, that marshal both children and teachers. As such, the internal culture of the school appears very different from the traditional model. It feels very unusual to be inside a school where there is time to complete a task, whether as a pupil or a teacher, and this creates a more human environment. A critical factor in these Minnesota schools is the training of teachers in 'responsive classroom practice', to enable them to develop skills and attitudes appropriate for teaching in a variety of ways dependent on the needs of the learners. In effect, teachers are taught how to teach students to

use space in their learning. One example, which has been operating for a decade, is the School of Environmental Sciences, known as the Zoo School, designed and built between 1993 and 1995. The school houses roughly 200 juniors and 200 seniors in a facility built on a 12-acre site on the grounds of the Minnesota Zoological gardens. The school is organized into two 'houses' and then into learning pods, within which approximately ten students have access to their own individual workspace and a shared conference table. The students decorate their individual and collective areas to reflect their identity. The pods are arranged around a large meeting space called a Centrum, where collective instruction happens. What few doors there are inside the building are seldom closed, and teaching staff eat alongside the students, creating a community of learners through such participative acts. This high school has been described as 'a junior school for big kids', maintaining much of the sense of home from home that is lost in many of the schools designed for older children.

Interior, The Zoo School, Minnesota, architect Bruce A. Jilk.

In the past, schools resembled one another. In England during the Victorian and Edwardian periods there was a distinct style that, in London at least, as we have seen, stemmed from the pen of one man, E. R. Robson. During the 1960s and '70s the possibilities that system building offered, and the pressure to build in quantity and with speed, led to a dominant style and a confidence in type. Since the 1990s there has been a clear shift towards designs that recognize local culture and heritage, and indeed that incorporate the historical and material resources of the locality.

In an earlier period of large-scale school rebuilding and refashioning, Eric Pearson argued that school design should ideally reflect the central triangle of human relationships that made a school function well. At that time, these were recognized as those between parent, child and teacher.[21] In the early 2000s the crucial principles of design for learning environments have emerged as the relationship between culture and ecology. In other words, school design is part of a complex interplay between individual, community and culture within a global context. Community has long been an important factor in considering the relationship between the internal life of a school and its immediate social locality, but today this is understood differently. The school building can demonstrate, for example in its choice of building materials or design features, a celebration of the skills and knowledge embedded in the culture of a community, implicitly challenging past injustices in relationships between different community groups.

René Dierkx, a Dutch architect engaged in participative design projects in Kenya, has drawn attention to the importance of place, identity and culture. He argues that it is 'important to develop and refine community-based architectural programming and school development methods, and to synthesize design, education and ecological knowledge in the development of school environments'.[22]

Dierkx has developed a process of community-based design for schools as 'inclusive learning environments' and 'child-friendly schools' in Nairobi's slums and in southern Sudan. School design workshops have encouraged children to express their needs for good learning environments. Their designs have suggested that their priorities were not so dissimilar from those in the most developed economies. They designed safe, healthy and inclusive schools. The crucial issues for these children revolved around the means of achieving survival in less than secure environments. One example reveals their priorities:

> The school is not secure because of the nearby factories, bars, and many destructive things . . . It is not very well ventilated and built. It is unsafe for the children because there are roads near and cars will easily knock down the children . . . The school does not have clean toilets. So, it makes the school have a bad aroma . . . It does not have trees, so it is very ugly and unwelcoming [Julia Muthoni, 13 years, Nairobi South Primary].[23]

Collaborative designs for inclusive and safe learning environments for the whole community have evolved from such discussions. For Dierkx, schools should recognize the contextual nature of learning,

Child Friendly School, Deng Nhial, Sudan, 2007. Rene Dierkx for UNICEF.

and should provide interventions that offer an alternative to street life and help to reintegrate children into society in productive, healthy ways. The designed learning environment should meet their basic needs for food, shelter and care, as well as offering personal development and opportunities for participation in the community. Its design should emphasize the interconnectedness of all life forms, emphasize the importance of the natural environment, and integrate classroom activities with exploration of the natural world. Such basic human needs are today often left behind in the rush towards the computer-driven learning environment. Dierkx's attention to the integration of ecological knowledge and cultural identity in design reflects a common concern among architects at this time. While knowledge, as traditionally conceived, appears to be fragile and lacks permanence, attention to local community-based cultural heritage, developed over centuries and communicated across generations, brings back a necessary permanence that reasserts itself in the form of community values and cultural identities.

The use of metaphor in school design is generating an approach to building that attempts to bring about harmony with the immediate cultural and ecological environment. Hence, for Zvi Hecker, architect of the Heinz Galinski School in Berlin, the overall designed form is both dynamic, reflecting energy and flow, and has significance as a political symbol celebrating cultural identity. Heinz Galinski is significant as the first school built for the Jewish community of Berlin since the end of the Second World War. Designed as a spiral, an unfolding book or the head of a sunflower as seen from above, the petals forming the classrooms, the form appears to prioritize the aesthetic over the functional. One is reminded of the basic geometric forms used by Friedrich Froebel (1782–1852), who, like Zvi Hecker, drew inspiration from the

Heinz Galinski school, Berlin, 1995; architect Zvi Hecker.

natural world in conceiving of the material structures known as 'gifts', which he believed would stimulate learning in young children. Hecker talks about his design as representing what already exists in the environment:

> The school is a city within a city. Its streets meet at squares and the squares become courtyards. The walls of the schoolhouse also build walkways, passages, and cul de sacs. The outside of the school is also the inside of the city, because the school is the city.[24]

In his design for Ingunnarskóli, a 'basic' or elementary school situated in Grafarholti, a new neighbourhood not far from the centre of Reykjavík, Bruce Jilk applied a particular approach to participative design in order to reveal the signs, symbols and metaphors clearly recognized in its landscape setting. The school was opened for its first intake in August 2005. Jilk uses the term 'design down' to describe the creative process by which this school

Heinz Galinski school.

emerged out of consultation with its users, the pupils, teachers and the wider community. Community, nature, spirit and flow were the crucial terms identified by the 'design down' committee through the initial consultations. These signify the unique cultural identity of the neighbourhood that the school serves. The design supports the many different possible uses of the space that might be expected to emerge over time through the commitment to such principles. The key element in the design is that it allows for a range of interpretations of use of space by children and teachers while suggesting certain possibilities. The 'intentional ambiguities' reflect a confidence in the creative response of children and teachers together designing through habitation. There are no classrooms as such but shared learning and teaching zones within each of the school's two stories. The interpretation of use of one of these zones in 2007 found 85

Ingunnarskoli, Reykjavik, Iceland, 2005; architect Bruce A. Jilk.

grade 5 and 6 students arranged in two equal sized groups with two main teachers attached. Fixed floor to ceiling storage cupboards with in-built 'wet area' facilities divide the area on either side of a performance / projection central space, used by all in the zone. Each half of the whole zone contains a soft area with cushions, sofa and parasol to create a space for escape, socialising or rest. There is no teacher's desk in the zone that is distinct from any other workspace. The large central lower storey space contains the school library, work spaces and a performance area.

Schools have been associated with learning and with the distribution of knowledge since the beginning of the modern period. Their presence has become part of the landscape, alongside other familiar institutions and community facilities such as shops, hospitals, factories and offices. New understandings of learning, however, and indeed new concepts of knowledge, together with technological advancements, have served to loosen the relationship between schools and learning, and to uncouple schools and buildings. Through advances in communications technologies, the modern school appears to be losing its credibility as the principal site of learning. Once again, the workplace and the home are becoming the locus for educational change and innovation.

In any era of large-scale rebuilding and change, with massive capital investment offered, there is a tendency to over-emphasize the role of design in influencing behaviour, thinking and being. There is often the strong suggestion, offered by the architectural profession, that a particular building design can answer all possible needs, now and in the foreseeable future. As Jilk has cautioned, educators and architects will do more for learners if they design less. He is convinced that the final shape and space of the school are dependent on its use by adults and children in the process of teaching and learning. In this sense, the school as a designed product should never be regarded as complete. It should be open to change and should offer 'disjunction' rather than conjunction between form and function. According to this view, in the past the formula of 'form follows function' has created its own monster, locking learning and teaching activities into predetermined spaces that meet the economic and political requirements of the providers first and the users second. In their 'over-design' of schools, architects have been guilty of a certain arrogance, believing that buildings alone can make a difference. According to Jilk, such 'over-design' inevitably leads to a renewed monumentalism. In spite of the constant messages of the importance of domestic scale received over time from those who have occupied the buildings, school design at the turn of the millennium tends to betray a renewed interest in the grand and the monumental, an emphasis on the view from the outside, atriums, symbols of renewal and progress.

Conclusion

Schools maintain their presence as significant and continuous features of the landscape in spite of advances in technology that appear to challenge their necessity in modern times. Both progressive educators and traditionalists draw attention to the design of schools as a crucial factor underpinning their ideology. Late in his life, the educator Paulo Freire addressed the relationship between progressive education and democracy, arguing that in the promotion of critical curiosity it was essential that due attention should be given to 'the educational space':

> Attention should go into every detail of the school space: hygiene, wall furnishings, cleanliness of desks, the teacher's desk setup, educational materials, books, magazines, newspapers, dictionaries, encyclopaedias . . . projectors, videos, fax, computers. By making clear that the educational space is valuable, the administration is able to demand the due respect from learners.[1]

Policies that promote the decentralization and democratization of the planning and design process and the forging of new partnerships in providing learning environments are, however, leading to a breakdown in the imagery associated with 'reading' a school referred to in the first few pages of this book. Schools may now appear anywhere and everywhere in the landscape of a city or countryside, in neighbourhoods or towns. Schools may occupy disused retail outlets, warehouses, museums or department stores. Today, one may pass by a high school on a city street without even noticing its presence, its security no longer ensured by gates and high fences but by a shroud of CCTV cameras. Yet one may still note a school in the landscape via the tell-tale signs of fences and gates, and one of the major challenges for planners in the twenty-first century is how to indicate in the architecture of a school an open and welcoming gesture to the community, while ensuring the security and safety of those within. In just over 100 years, security concerns have shifted from the perceived need to keep pupils in to the need to keep intruders out. The values of accessibility, user-friendliness and inclusion promoted by modern governmental policies can therefore clash directly with concerns for safety, security and surveillance. Although democratic values of freedom of expression, rights and responsibilities and the associated critical and creative faculties are celebrated within emerging curricula, it is not clear how these values can be signified in the built environment. Architects are critical partners in realizing this objective. As in the past, they can block, be neutral or facilitate a learner's engagement, depending on their willingness and ability to share authority with pupils and teachers in the design process of the learning environment.

Some years ago, the American poet and writer Philip Lopate drew attention to the ubiquitous school building of modern urban societies that was largely taken for granted:

> It might just as well be invisible. Most neighbourhood people don't even see it. Three stories high, built of administrative red brick, as easily mistaken for a bus depot as a public school, it seems to urge you not

to notice it, like a stalled driver who waves the other cars past . . . the building must once have been spanking new. It must once have been a lightning-rod connecting all the high-minded hopes of parents and community who had to exert incalculable pressure on city officials to get it built.[2]

Schools are at one and the same time cherished and overlooked as emblems of civil life, as markers of progress, and as statements of hope for the future. Most people living in the wealthier parts of the world regard school as a normal, everyday part of being a child and growing up. Yet at the same time school design continues to demand the utmost dedication from individual educators, architects, children, teachers and members of the community in realizing its usefulness and fitness for imparting the new knowledge to future generations. For the foreseeable years to come, schools will continue to alter and develop according to the contours of policy, economics, demographics and aesthetics. Their design and redesign, however, will struggle to be free of the historical dimension that so characterizes their place in memory and in the landscape.

References

Introduction

1 Quoted in Amy S. Weisser, '"Little Red School House, What Now?": Two Centuries of American Public School Architecture', *Journal of Planning History*, V/3 (2006), p. 196.

2 Thomas A. Markus, *Buildings and Power: Freedom and Control in the Origin of Modern Building Types* (London, 1993).

3 C. M. Fitz, 'The Learning Environment as Place: An Analysis of the USA Department of Education's Six Design Principles for Learning Environments', unpublished MSc. thesis, Washington State University, Vancouver, 2003.

4 George Godwin, *Town Swamps and Social Bridges* (London, 1859), pp. 94–5.

5 J. Pollack, *Educating the Youth of Pennsylvania: Worlds of Learning in the Age of Franklin* (Philadephia, PA, 2006).

6 D. B. Tyack, 'The One Best System: A History of American Urban Education', in *Building and Learning: New Schools for New York*, ed. A. Reiselbach (New York, 1992), p. 164.

7 H. Cunningham, *Children and Childhood in Western Society since 1500* (London, 1995), pp. 157–9.

8 H. S. Bowles and H. Gintis, *Schooling in Capitalist America* (London, 1976), p. 153.

9 George Copa, 'The Comprehensive High School as a Context for Vocational Education: An Historic Perspective', presented at the annual meeting of the American Vocational Education Research Association, Anaheim, CA, 3–6 December 1983.

10 Sarah Hill, School Works Report (February 2007), at www.school-works.org/

11 See Jane Havell and Peter Sidler, eds, *Kid Size: The Material World of Childhood* (Weil am Rhein, 1997); and C. Wilk, ed., *Modernism: Designing a New World, 1914–1939* (London, 2006).

12 Quoted in Galen Cranz, *The Chair: Rethinking Culture, Body and Design* (New York, 1998), p. 62.

13 See Ian Grosvenor, '"The Art of Seeing": Promoting Design in Education in 1930s

England', *Paedagogica Historica*, XLI/4–5 (2005), pp. 507–34.

14 Reyner Banham, 'The Architecture of the English School: Essay Review of Malcolm Seaborne and Roy Lowe, *The English School: Its Architecture and Organization. Volume II: 1870–1970*', *History of Education Quarterly*, XXI/2 (1981), pp. 189–93.

1 Beacons of Civilization

1 E. R. Robson, *School Architecture* [1874] (Leicester, 1972).

2 Arthur Conan Doyle, 'The Naval Treaty', in *The Memoirs of Sherlock Holmes* (Harmondsworth, 1950), p. 215.

3 Agustín Escolano Benito, 'The School in the City: School Architecture as Discourse and as Text', *Paedagogica Historica*, XXXIX/1–2 (2003), p. 60; Antonio Viñao, 'The School Head's Office as Territory and Place: Location and Physical Layout in the First Spanish Graded Schools', in *Materialities of Schooling*, ed. Martin Lawn and Ian Grosvenor (Oxford, 2005), pp. 47–70; Frank Irving Cooper, 'The Planning of School Houses', *American Architect*, 96 (17 November 1909), pp. 189–90; and A. D. Hamlin, 'Consideration in School House Design', *American Architect*, 96 (17 November 1909), p. 192.

4 *Reports from the Select Committee on the Education of Lower Orders in the Metropolis: Third Report* (London, 1816); Werner Moser, 'La escuela en la cuidad', *Revista de arquitectura contemporanea*, XI (1933), p. 28.

5 J.N.L. Durand, *Précis des leçons d'architecture* [1802], quoted in Adrian Forty, *Words and Buildings: A Vocabulary of Modern Architecture* (London, 2002), p. 79.

6 See, for example, Jane McGregor and Doreen Massey, 'Space and Schools', special issue of *Forum*, XLVI/1 (2004).

7 P. B. Cliffe, *The Rise and Development of the Sunday School Movement in England, 1780–1880* (Redhill, 1986).

8 Charles Dickens, *The Letters of Charles Dickens*, ed. Madeline House and Graham Storey, 12 vols (Oxford, 1965–2002), III, pp. 562–4.

9 C. J. Montague, *Sixty Years in Waifdom; or, The Ragged School Movement in English History* (London, 1904).

10 Kathryn Morrison, *The Workhouse: A Study of Poor-Law Buildings in England* (Swindon, 1999), especially pp. 132–54.

11 Thomas Wood, 'The Autobiography of Thomas Wood, 1822–1880', quoted in David Vincent, *Bread, Knowledge and Freedom: A Study of Nineteenth-Century Working Class Autobiography* (London, 1981), p. 99.

12 Vincent, *Bread, Knowledge and Freedom*, p. 101.

13 Neil Jackson, 'School', Grove Art Online: www.groveart.com/shared/views/article.html?section=art.076757.2 (accessed 7 June 2007).

14 Roger Dixon and Stefan Muthesius, *Victorian Architecture* (London, 1978), pp. 236–7.

15 See Thomas A. Markus, *Buildings and Power: Freedom and Control in the Origin of Modern Building Types* (London, 1993), pp. 48–69, for a detailed discussion of the Bell and Lancaster systems.

16 Thomas Dunning, 'Reminiscences of Thomas Dunning [*c*. 1890]', quoted in Vincent, *Bread, Knowledge and Freedom*, p. 97.

17 Samuel Wilderspin, *On the Importance of Educating the Infant Children of the Poor* (London, 1823), pp. 18–19.

18 Samuel Wilderspin, *Early Discipline Illustrated; or, The Infant System Progressing and Successful* (London, 1832), pp. 5–6.

19 John Stow, *The Training System Adopted in Model Schools of the Glasgow Educational Society* (Glasgow, 1836), p. 69.

20 Samuel Wilderspin, *On the Importance of Educating the Infant Children of the Poor*, 2nd edn (London, 1824), p. 171; Select Committee evidence quoted in Ian Hunter, *Rethinking the School* (St Leonards, 1994), pp. 72–3.

21 Stow, *The Training System Adopted in Model Schools of the Glasgow Educational Society*, p. 135.

22 See Malcolm Seaborne, *The English School: Its Architecture and Organisation, 1370–1870* (Toronto, 1971), chapter 8; Markus, *Buildings and Power*, especially chapter 3.

23 H. Barnard, *School Architecture* (New York, 1838); Dell Upton, 'Lancastrian Schools, Republican Citizenship and the Spatial Imagination in Early Nineteenth Century America', *Journal of the Society of Architectural Historians*, LV/3 (1996), pp. 238–53; R. Rayman, 'Joseph Lancaster's Monitorial System of Instruction and American Indian Education, 1815–1838', *History of Education Quarterly*, XXI/4 (1981), pp. 395–409.

24 Henry Barnard, *School Architecture* (New York, 1838), p. 23.

25 Robson, *School Architecture*, p. 72.

26 Ibid., p. 71.

27 Jackson, 'School', Grove Art Online: www.groveart.com/shared/views/ article.html?section=art.076757.2.

28 Robson, *School Architecture*, p. 2.

29 F. Narjoux, *Ecoles primaries et salles d'aisles: construction et installation* (Paris, 1879); K. Hintrager, *Volksschulhauser in Schweden, Norwegen, Danemark und Finland* (1895), and Hintrager, *Volksschulhauser in Oesterreich-Ungarn, Bosnien und der Hercegovina* (1901).

30 Robson, *School Architecture*, p. 71.

31 Ibid., p. 22.

32 Ibid., pp. 1–2.

33 Reyner Banham, 'The Architecture of the English School: Essay Review of Malcolm Seaborne and Roy Lowe, *The English School: Its Architecture and Organization. Volume II: 1870–1970*', *History of Education Quarterly*, XXI/2 (1981), pp. 189–93.

34 J. F. Moss, *Notes on National Education in Continental Europe* (London, 1873), p. 18.

35 Kevin J. Brehony, ed., *The Origins of Nursery Education: Freidrich Froebel and the English System*, 6 vols (London, 2001); R. L. Wollens, ed., *Kindergartens and Cultures: The Global Diffusion of an Idea* (New Haven, CT, 2000).

36 Robson, *School Architecture*, pp. 77–86; Heidemarie Kemnitz, 'Elementarschulen in Deutschland und ihre Gebäude: Das Beispiel Berlin', in *Prinz Albert und die Ent-wicklung des Bildungswesens in England und Deutschland*, ed. F. Bosbach, W. Filmer-Sankey and H. Hiery (Munich, 2000), pp. 53–62.

37 Moss, *Notes on National Education in Continental Europe*, p. 33.

38 Ibid., p. 31.

39 See Ellwood Cubberly, *Public Education in the United States: A Study and Interpretation of American Educational History* (Boston, MA, 1934).

40 Robson, *School Architecture*, p. 27.

41 Ibid., pp. 27–46; E. M. Bacon, *Boston Illustrated* (Boston, MA, 1872).

42 Robson, *School Architecture*, pp. 1–2, 6–7, 160.

43 Dixon and Muthesius, *Victorian Architecture*, pp. 239–40.

44 Catherine Burke and Ian Grosvenor, 'Designed Spaces, Disciplined Bodies: E. R. Robson's Grand Architectural Tour', in *Cultuuroverdracht als pedagogisch motief*, ed. G. Timmerman, N. Baker and J. Dekker (Groningen, 2007), pp. 39–54. For the style generally, see Mark Girouard, *Sweetness and Light: The 'Queen Anne' Movement, 1860–1900* (Oxford, 1977).

45 Patrick Joyce, *The Rule of Freedom* (London, 2003), pp. 144–82. See M. Schwarzer, *German Architectural Theory and the Search for Modernity* (Cambridge, 1995).

46 Quoted in Malcolm Seaborne and Roy Lowe, *The English School: Its Architecture and Organisation. Volume II: 1870–1970* (London, 1977), p. 26.

47 Robson, *School Architecture*, p. 169.

48 Ibid., p. 216.

49 Birmingham Central Library, Archives Department: Sapcote Building Records; Sherbourne Road School archives.

50 Ibid.

51 Cyril Norwood and Arthur Hope, *The Higher Education of Boys in England* (London, 1909), pp. 79 and 111.

52 Birmingham Central Library, Archives Department: Sapcote Building Records; Sherbourne Road School archives. Organisation for Economic Co-operation and Development, *Schools for Today and Tomorrow* (Paris, 1996), pp. 74–7, 86–8.

53 Information from Willi Brand and Ingrid Lohmann. See also Hermann Lange, *Schulbau und Schulfassung der frühen Neuzeit* (Berlin, 1967).

54 See Ian Grosvenor and Martin Lawn, 'In Search of the School', *Bildung und Erziehung*, LIV/1 (2001), pp. 55–70.

55 David Hutchison, *A Natural History of Place in Education* (New York, 2004), p. 50.

56 Thomas A. Markus, 'Early Nineteenth Century School Space and Ideology', *Paedagogica Historica*, XXX/2 (1996), p. 12.

57 D. H. Lawrence, *The Rainbow* (Harmondsworth, 1949), p. 379.

2 The School of Tomorrow

1 John Dewey, *The School and Society, and the Child and the Curriculum*, ed. Philip W. Jackson (Chicago, IL, 1990), pp. 31–3.
2 Jan Molema, quoted in Mark Dudek, *Architecture of Schools: The New Learning Environments* (Oxford, 2000), p. 27.
3 H. Myles Wright and R. Gardner-Medwin, *The Design of Nursery and Elementary Schools* (London, 1938), p. 109.
4 John Dewey, *The Child and the Curriculum* (Chicago, IL, 1920), p. 52.
5 National Archives, E21849: Unsatisfactory Public Elementary Schools (1912).
6 Moreno Martinez, 'History of School Desk Development in Terms of Hygiene and Pedagogy in Spain (1838–1936)', in Martin Lawn and Ian Grosvenor, eds, *Materialities of Schooling* (Oxford, 2005) p. 75.
7 *New York Times* (4 June 1921).
8 Lord Bishop of Ripon, Vice-President of the Infant Mortality Conferences, 1906 and 1908; quoted in Harry Hendrick, *Child Welfare* (Bristol, 2003), p. 86.
9 Ralph H. Crowley, *The Hygiene of School Life* (London, 1910), p. 330.
10 Ralph H. Crowley, *Report to the Board of Education: School Hygiene and Medical Inspection in US and Canada* (London, April 1914).
11 Ralph H. Crowley and Hilda Wilson, *The School System of Gary Indiana* (London, 1914), p. 207.
12 Ralph H. Crowley, *Report on the Fourth International Congress on School Hygiene at Buffalo, USA, 1913*, p. 15.
13 Crowley and Wilson, *The School System of Gary Indiana*, p. 207.
14 Crowley, *Report on the Fourth International Congress on School Hygiene*.
15 Ralph H. Crowley, *Child Guidance Clinics: With Special Reference to the American Experience* (London, 1928).
16 Ralph H. Crowley, 'An Address to the Friends Guild of Teachers, Letchworth', *The Friends Quarterly Examiner* (January 1935).
17 'Obituary notice: R. H. Crowley', *The Lancet* (10 October 1953).
18 Ralph H. Crowley, 'The Mental Health of the Child', paper presented to the Federation of Education Committees Conference, London, 2 June 1933.
19 Margaret McMillan, *The Nursery School* (London, 1919), p. 270. See also Mark Dudek, *Kindergarten Architecture* (London, 1996), p. 31.
20 Willem van der Eyken and Barry Turner, *Adventures in Education* (London, 1969), p. 104.
21 Beatrice Ensor, 'Schools of To-morrow', *New Era* 6, 23 (1925), pp. 81–7; Joy Elmer Morgan, 'The School of To-morrow', *New Era* (April 1927), pp. 44–5; Beryl Parker, '"But Everywhere Schools Are Different"', *New Era* (April 1927), pp. 9–43.
22 Andrew Saint, *Towards a Social Architecture: The Role of School Building in Post-War England* (New Haven, CT, 1987), p. 39.
23 Neil Jackson, 'School', Grove Art Online: www.groveart.com/shared/views/article.html?section=art.076757.2 (accessed 7 June 2007).

24 Macmillan, *The Nursery School*, p. 271.

25 Felix Clay, *Modern School Buildings Elementary and Secondary* (London, 1902), p. 172.

26 Philip Robson, *School Planning* (London, 1911), p. 15.

27 C. G. Stillman, *The Modern School* (London, 1949), pp. 28, 33 and 38.

28 Eckhardt Fuchs, 'Educational Sciences, Morality and Politics: International Educational Congresses in the Early Twentieth Century', *Paedagogica Historica*, XL/5–6 (2004), pp. 757–84.

29 Thomas Schumacher, *The Danteum: Architecture, Poetics and Politics under Italian Fascism* (New York, 1985), p. 31. See also T. Schumacher, *Surface and Symbol: Guiseppe Terragni and the Architecture of Italian Rationalism* (New York, 1991).

30 Rayner Banham, *The Age of the Masters: A Personal View of Modern Architecture* (New York, 1975), p. 91.

31 Ken Worpole, 'Architecture, Landscape and the Social Democratic Sublime': www.worpole.dircon.co.uk/show_soc_dem_sublime.html (accessed December 2005).

32 Ken Worpole, *Here Comes the Sun: Architecture and Public Space in Twentieth-Century European Culture* (London, 2000), p. 14.

33 Anne-Marie Châtelet, Dominique Lerch and Jean-Noël Luc, *L'école de plein air: une expérience pédagogique et architecturale dans l'Europe du XXième siècle* (Paris, 2003), p. 34.

34 Roy Lowe, 'The Educational Impact of the Eugenics Movement', *International Journal of Educational Research*, III/2 (1998), p. 658.

35 Ian Grosvenor and Kevin Myers, 'Progressivism, Control and Correction: Local Education Authorities and Educational Policy in 20th Century England', *Paedagogica Historica*, XLII/1–2 (2006), pp. 225–48.

36 Macmillan, *The Nursery School*, p. 322.

37 Amy S. Weisser, '"Little Red School House, What Now?" Two Centuries of American Public School Architecture', *Journal of Planning History*, V/3 (2006), pp. 204–6.

38 William Greeley, 'The Fourth Dimension in Schoolhouse Design', *Architectural Forum*, XXXVI (1922), pp. 129–30.

39 See www.rosenwaldschools.com

40 Saint, *Towards a Social Architecture*, p. 36.

41 Jackson, 'School', Grove Art Online: www.groveart.com/shared/views/article.html?section=art.076757.2 (accessed 7 June 2007).

42 Charlotte Benton, *A Different World: Emigré Architects in Britain, 1928–1958* (London, 1995), p. 230. Benton identified 60 such émigré architects who sought refuge between 1931 and 1939.

43 Ian Grosvenor, '"The Art of Seeing": Promoting Design in Education in 1930s England', *Paedagogica Historica*, XLI/4–5 (2005), pp. 507–34.

44 Harry Rée, *Educator Extraordinary: The Life and Achievement of Henry Morris* (London, 1985), pp. 70–71.

45 Henry Morris, *The Village College: Being a Memorandum on the Provision of Educational and Social Facilities for the Countryside, with Special Reference to Cambridgeshire* (Cambridge, 1925).

46 Grosvenor, '"The Art of Seeing"', p. 522.

47 Herbert Read, *Education through Art* (London, 1943), pp. 290–95. The book was reprinted four times before 1946.

48 Maxwell Fry, *Fine Building* (London, 1944), p. 77.

49 Grosvenor, '"The Art of Seeing"', p. 522.

50 Benton, *A Different World*, p. 55.

51 *Birmingham Post* (8 January 1937).

52 Quoted in Stuart Maclure, *Educational Developments and School Building: Aspects of Public Policy, 1945–73* (London, 1984), p. 6.

53 H. Becker, 'School Buildings in Modern Society', in *School Buildings*, ed. K. Otto (London, 1966), pp. 11–16.

54 Catherine Burke, '"The School Without Tears": E. F. O'Neill of Prestolee', *History of Education*, XXXIV/3 (2005), pp. 263–75.

55 Alfred Oftedal and Tedal Telhaug, 'From Collectivism to Individualism? Education as Nation Building in a Scandinavian Perspective', *Scandinavian Journal of Educational Research*, XLVIII/2 (2004), p. 5.

56 William Beveridge 'New Britain', in *Pillars of Security and Other War-Time Addresses* (London, 1942), pp. 80–81.

57 Catherine Burke and Ian Grosvenor, *The School I'd Like: Children and Young People's Reflections on an Education for the 21st Century* (London, 2003), pp. 3–4.

58 *Architectural Design*, XXIX (June 1959), p. 219.

59 Ron Ringshall, 'Education Buildings in Inner London', in *The Urban School: Buildings for Education in London, 1870–1980*, ed. R. Ringshall, M. Miles and F. Kelsall (London, 1983), p. 49.

60 Birmingham Central Library, Archives Department, Miscellaneous Education files, Central Council for Health Education, 1947.

61 Maclure, *Educational Developments and School Building*, p. 40.

62 Ibid., p. 27.

63 Saint, *Towards a Social Architecture*, p. 55.

64 *The Story of a School: A Headmaster's Experiences with Children Aged Seven to Eleven* (London, 1949).

65 Van der Eyken and Turner, *Adventures in Education*, p. 114.

66 Maclure, *Educational Developments and School Building*, p. 41.

67 David Hutchison, *A Natural History of Place in Education* (New York, 2004), pp. 53–4; Alfred Roth, *The New School* (Zurich, 1961).

68 Van der Eyken and Turner, *Adventures in Education*, p. 118.

69 Alan Powers, *Britain* (London, 2007), p.50.

70 Jackson, 'School', Grove Art Online: www.groveart.com/shared/views/
   article.html?section=art.076757.2 (accessed 7 June 2007).
71 Saint, *Towards a Social Architecture*, p. 62.
72 R. Llewelyn-Davies and J. R. Weekes, 'The Hertfordshire Achievement',
   Architectural Review, 144 (June 1952), pp. 367–87.
73 Walter Gropius, 'Gropius Apprises Today's Architects', *Architectural Forum*
   (May 1952), pp. 111, 166, 178 and 182.
74 *Architectural Review*, 112 (July 1952), pp. 30–37.
75 T. Dannatt, *Modern British Architecture* (London, 1959), p. 19.
76 Elain Harwood 'A Gazetteer of Buildings in the London Area', in *A Different
   World*, p. 134.
77 G. E. Kidder Smith, *The New Architecture of Europe* (London, 1962), p. 35.
78 Powers, *Britain*, p. 98.
79 *Education* (29 October 1954), p. 658.
80 *Architects Journal* (16 September 1954), p. 336.
81 Kidder Smith, *The New Architecture of Europe*, pp. 57–8.
82 Ibid., p. 65; 'The Village School, Little Wymondley', *Architectural Review*, CXII
   (1952), pp. 76–81.
83 Kidder Smith, *The New Architecture of Europe*, pp. 50–52.
84 Ibid., p. 36.
85 Dudek, *Architecture of Schools*, p. 32.
86 Ibid., p. 30; Richards quoted in Reyner Banham, 'The Architecture of the English
   School: Essay Review of Malcolm Seaborne and Roy Lowe, *The English School:
   Its Architecture and Organization. Volume II: 1870–1970*', *History of Education
   Quarterly*, XXI/2 (1981), p. 190.
87 M. Lawn, 'Postwar Schooling', unpublished paper (2005).
88 Department of Education and Science, *The School Building Survey* (London,
   1962).
89 Malcolm Seaborne, *Primary School Design* (London, 1971), p. 75.
90 *Education* (30 July 1954).
91 Grosvenor, '"The Art of Seeing"', p. 517.
92 Rée, *Educator Extraordinary*, pp. 103–4; Read, *Education Through Art*, pp. 291–2.

3 The 'Expanding School' and the 'Exploding Classroom'

1 C. G. Stillman and R. Castle-Cleary, *The Modern School* (London, 1949), p. 49.
2 Carlo Testa, *New Educational Facilities* (Boulder, CO, 1975).
3 Ibid., pp. 50–53.
4 Eileen Molony, *The Expanding Classroom* (London, 1969). The objective of this
   BBC television series was to provide an explanation or illustration of how
   'Britain's progressive active classrooms' work and to demonstrate some of the
   attempts to move over from subject-centred to child-centred education.

5 Philip Toogood, *The Head's Tale* (Telford, 1984); A. H. Halsey, *Educational Priority, Volume 1: EPA Problems and Policies* (London, 1972), p. 79.

6 Peter Blundell Jones, *Hans Scharoun* (London, 1995), p. 28.

7 Ibid., p. 150.

8 Peter Blundell Jones, 'Sharoun, Hans', Grove Art Online: www.groveart.com/shared/views/article.html?from=search&section=art.076418 (accessed 18 June 2007).

9 For a full, illustrated discussion of the school at Lunen, see Heidemarie Kemnitz, 'Schulbau jenseits der Norm: Hans Scharouns Madchengymnasium in Lunen', *Paedagogica Historica*, XLI/4–5 (August 2005), pp. 605–25.

10 Malcolm Seaborne, *Primary School Design* (London, 1971).

11 George Baines, 'Social and Environmental Studies', in *Teaching in the British Primary School*, ed. Vincent R. Rogers (London, 1970), pp. 199–216.

12 John Holt, 'Children Are Sensitive to Space', in *Learning Environments*, ed. Thomas G. David and B. D. Wright (Chicago, IL, and London, 1975).

13 Barbara Villet, 'The Children Want Classrooms Alive with Chaos', n.d., published article in George Baines Archive, Institute of Education, London.

14 Andrew Saint, *Towards a Social Architecture* (London, 1987), p. 213.

15 The Plowden Report, *Children and Their Primary Schools* (London, 1967), p. 396.

16 Edith Moorhouse, *A Personal Story of Oxfordshire Primary Schools, 1956–1968* (London, 1988), p. 41.

17 Ibid., p. 57.

18 Ibid., p. 61.

19 Eric Pearson, *Trends in School Design* (London, 1972), pp. 26–8.

20 Ibid., p. 76.

21 George Baines, 'Learning in a Flexible School', in *The Integrated Day on Theory and Practice*, ed. Jack Walton (London, 1971), p. 34.

22 Sarah Aitcheson, 'Eynsham School and the Progressive Experiment, 1967–1983', unpublished MA dissertation, Institute of Education, London (2004), p. 34.

23 Journal of Judith E. Purbook, who was deputy head teacher at Eynsham and was later to become Judith Baines through marriage to George Baines. George Baines archive, Institute of Education, London.

24 The Plowden Report, *Children and their Primary Schools*, was published in 1967. The report surveyed the state of primary education in England and Wales and recognized innovation in educational design.

25 David Medd, memo, Institute of Education Architecture and Buildings Archive, 307/29 (File 28).

26 David Medd, *School Furniture* (Paris, 1981).

27 Saint, *Towards a Social Architecture*.

28 Neil Jackson, 'School', Grove Art Online: www.groveart.com/shared/views/article.html?section=art.076757.3 (accessed 7 June 2007).

29 Michael Hacker of the Architects and Buildings Branch, Ministry of Education, cited in Saint, *Towards a Social Architecture*, p. 196.

30 Scotland had always adopted comprehensive organization of state education, as had much of Wales.

31 Stewart C. Mason, *In Our Experience: The Changing Schools of Leicestershire* (London, 1970).

32 Tim McMullen, in *The Countesthorpe Experience: The First Five Years*, ed. J. Watts (London, 1977).

33 Brian Simon, in *The Countesthorpe Experience*, ed. Watts, pp. 18–19.

34 Nikolaus Pevsner, *London: The Cities of London and Westminster*, 3rd edn, revised by Bridget Cherry (Harmondsworth, 1973), p. 515.

35 Two volumes of the Black Papers were published by the Critical Quarterly Society. Vol. I, C. B. Cox (compiler), K. Amis and A. E. Dyson, 'Fight for Education: A Black Paper', January 1968, London. Vol. ii, C. B. Cox and A. E. Dyson, 'The Crisis in Education: Black Paper 2', 1970, London.

36 Colin Ward, ed., *British School Buildings: Designs and Appraisals, 1964–74* (London, 1976), pp. 51–62.

37 Malcolm Seaborne, *Primary School Design* (London, 1971).

4 Aligning Architecture and Education – Building Schools 'That Fit'

1 Tracy Kidder, *Among Schoolchildren* (London, 1991); cited in Mike Davies, 'Less Is More: The Move to Person-Centred, Human Scale Education', *Forum*, XLVII/2–3 (2005), pp. 97–101.

2 David Halpin, *Hope and Education: The Role of the Utopian Imagination* (London, 2003).

3 Davies, 'Less is More'.

4 Michael Fielding, 'Leadership, Personalization and High Performance Schooling: Naming the New Totalitarianism', *School Leadership and Management*, XXVI/4 (September 2006), p. 350.

5 RIBA East Architecture for Education Award 2005: www.riba.org/go/RIBA/About/RIBAEast_2901.html (accessed 18 June 2007).

6 Peter Hübner, *Kinder bauen ihre Schule: Evangelische Gesamtschule Gelsenkirchen* (Stuttgart and London, 2005), p. 7.

7 Davis, 'Less is More', p. 102.

8 See www.school-works.org.

9 School Works National Online Poll Report, February 2006, p. 7: www.school-works.org/

10 Alison Clark, Anne Trine Kjørholt and Peter Moss, eds, *Beyond Listening: Children's Perspectives on Early Childhood Services* (London, 2005).

11 'Making Space: Architecture and Design for Young Children', *Children in Europe*, 8 (April 2005), pp. 22–3.

12 See, for example, John Eberhard at *www.architecture-mind.com/*

13 Roger Hart, cited in Catherine Burke and Ian Grosvenor, *The School I'd Like:*

Children and Young People's Reflections on an Education for the 21st Century (London, 2003), p. 31.

14 Peter Hübner, *Kinder bauen ihre Schule*, p. 7.

15 Burke and Grosvenor, *The School I'd Like*, p. 17.

16 David Orr, 'What Is Education For? Six Myths about the Foundations of Modern Education, and Six New Principles To Replace Them', *In Context* (1991): www.context.org/ICLIB/IC27/Orr.htm (accessed November 2005).

17 P. Blundell Jones, *Peter Hübner: Building as a Social Process* (Stuttgart and London, 2007), p. 149.

18 'Capital City Academy, London, UK, 2000–2003': www.fosterandpartners.com/Projects/1128/Default.aspx (accessed 18 June 2007).

19 Hilary Wilce, 'On Shaky Foundations', *The Independent*, Education supplement (21 September 2006), p. 4.

20 For Stonebridge, see www.stillwater.k12.mn.us/sb/sb (accessed September 2006).

21 Eric Pearson, *Trends in School Design* (Basingstoke and London, 1972), p. 14.

22 Rene Dierkx, 'Development of Inclusive Learning Environments in Nairobi's Slums', *Children, Youth and Environments*, XIII/1 (Spring 2003).

23 Quoted in ibid.

24 Zvi Hecker, 'The Heinz Galinski School, Berlin, Germany': www.arcspace.com/architects/zvi_hecker/heinz_galinski/index.htm (accessed 18 June 2007).

5 Conclusion

1 Paulo Freire, *Pedagogy of the Heart* (New York, 2003), p. 97.

2 Philip Lopate, *Being With Children* (New York, 1973).

Select Bibliography

Barnard, H., *School Architecture; or, Contributions to the Improvement of School-Houses in the United States* (New York, 1848)

Benton, Charlotte, *A Different World: Emigré Architects in Britain, 1928–1958* (London, 1995)

Burke, Catherine, and Ian Grosvenor, *The School I'd Like: Children and Young People's Reflections on an Education for the 21st Century* (London, 2002)

Clay, Felix, *Modern School Buildings: Elementary and Secondary* (London, 1902)

Dudek, Mark, *Architecture of Schools: The New Learning Environments* (Oxford, 2000)

Jelich, Franz-Josef, and Heidemarie Kemnitz, *Die pädagogische Gestaltung des Raums: Geschichte und ModerModernität* (Klinkhardt, 2003)

Kristenson, Hjördis, *Skolhuset: Idé och form* (Stockholm, 2005)

Maclure, Stuart, *Educational Developments and School Building: Aspects of Public Policy, 1945–73* (London, 1984)

Markus, Thomas A., *Buildings and Power: Freedom and Control in the Origin of Modern Building Types* (London, 1993)

Pearson, Eric, *Trends in School Design* (Basingstoke and London, 1972)

Robson, E. R., *School Architecture* [1874] (Leicester, 1972)

Roth, Alfred, *The New School* (Zurich, 1961)

Saint, Andrew, *Towards a Social Architecture: The Role of School Building in Post-War England* (New Haven, CT, 1987)

Seaborne, Malcolm, *The English School: Its Architecture and Organisation, 1370–1870* (London, 1971)

–, *Primary School Design* (London, 1971)

–, and Roy Lowe, *The English School: Its Architecture and Organisation. Volume II: 1870–1970* (London, 1977)

Stillman, C. G., *The Modern School* (London, 1949)

Ward, Colin, ed., *British School Buildings Designs and Appraisals, 1964–74* (London, 1976)

Acknowledgements

Research always has the potential to be collaborative and we have particularly benefited from the knowledge and insights of George and Judith Baines, Willi Brand, Ron Butchart, Paulo Catrica, Craig Campbell, Karl Catteeuw, Ning De Conick-Smith, Mineke van Essen, Catherine Mary Fritz, Claire Gallagher, Pete James, Heidmarie Kemnitz, Leena Kaikkonen, Michael Søgaard Larsen, Martin Lawn, Reiner Lehberger, Ingrid Lohmann, Charles Magnin, Christine Mayer, David Medd, Ulrike Mietzner, Stephen Mosley, Antonio Novoa, Pablo Pineau, John Pollack, Elsie Rockwell, Kate Rousmaniere, Carmen Sanchidrian, Frank Simon and Harry Smaller.

Thanks to Rita McLean, Siân Roberts, Judy Torrington and Bruce Jilk for reading drafts; Peter Blundell-Jones for photographs and comments; Richard Angelo, Frank Stanger and Caroline Baxter for locating images, and Sarah Aitchison, Institute of Education archives, and Brigitte Winsor, Birmingham Central Library, for specialist advice.

Photographic Acknowledgements

The author and publishers wish to express their thanks to the below sources of illustrative material and/or permission to reproduce it:

The Architectural Review (Galwey, Arphot): pp. 106, 107, 108, 111, 112, 113, 148; from *Art Journal* (1881): p. 29; photo Birmingham City Archives/Birmingham Central Library Local Studies Department: pp. 58, 82 (right), 83; photos Peter Blundell-Jones: pp. 122, 169, 171; image by Sam Booth, for 'School Works', from *A–Z Sketchbook of School Build and Design*, courtesy Sam Booth: p. 168; from Burke and Grosvenor, *The School I'd Like* (2003): p. 170; Crown Copyright: p. 97 (top); photo Mike Davies: p. 157; photo Kahryn Ferry/The Victorian Society: p. 27; photo London Metropolitan Archives: p. 150; photo Andrea Gottschalk: p. 18; photos Ian Grosvenor: pp. 9, 14 (top), 15, 16, 64, 78 (right), 97 (middle); photos courtesy Zvi Hecker: pp. 182, 183; Institute of Education Archives, London: pp. 98, 99; Institute of Education, University of London (Papers of George and Judith Baines), courtesy George and Judith Baines: pp. 128, 137, 139; Institute of Education, University of London (Medd Collection): pp. 133 (middle), 144; photo courtesy Bruce A. Jilk: p. 178; photo courtesy Bruce A. Jilk/Rene Dierkx: p. 180; photo Svanborg R. Jónsdóttir: p. 184; Heidemarie Kemnitz: p. 125; photo Martine Hamilton Knight Photography: p. 167; photos David Medd: pp. 133 (foot), 134, 141, 142, 143; from *Minutes of the Committee of Council on Education* (1840): p. 35; Musée National de l'Education, Paris: p. 39; Nationaal Schoolmuseum, Rotterdam: pp. 82 (left), 94; from *The New Era* (1927): p. 75; photos courtesy Norman Foster Group: pp. 6, 175; photos John D. Prosser: pp. 155, 156; from H. Read, *Education through Art* (1943): p. 89; from E. R. Robson, *School Architecture* (1874): pp. 34 (top right), 47, 48, 54, 55, 60; from Alfred Roth, *The New School* (1961) pp. 100, 101; photo Carmen Sanchidrian: p. 12; photo Rachel Sayers: p. 161 (bottom left); from G. C. Stillman and R. Castle Cleary, *The Modern School* (1949): pp. 53, 81, 84 (top), 110, 163; photo Terragni Foundation, Como: p. 79; University of Kentucky Library University Archives (Cora Wilson Stewart Collection): p. 63; photo Rob Walker: p. 34 (top left); from Samuel Wilderspin, *A System for the Education of the Young . . .* (1840): p. 37; photo William Wollaston, Birmingham City Archives/Birmingham Central Library Local Studies Department: p. 56; photos Larraine and Ken Worpole: pp. 68, 80; photo Michele Zini/Adam Nieman: p. 161 (bottom right); photo Michele Zini/Martine Hamilton Knight: p. 165.

Index